PATTERNS 2023

The Fifteenth International Conferences on Pervasive Patterns and Applications

June 26 - 30, 2023

Nice, France

PATTERNS 2023 Editors

Jens Weber, Baden-Wuerttemberg Cooperative State University Loerrach and Mercedes-Benz AG, Germany

Jan Spoor, Karlsruhe Institute of Technology and Mercedes-Benz AG, Germany

Printed from e-media with permission by:

Curran Associates, Inc.
57 Morehouse Lane
Red Hook, NY 12571

Some format issues inherent in the e-media version may also appear in this print version.

International Academy, Research, and Industry Association (IARIA)
412 Derby Way
Wilmington, DE 19810

Phone: (408) 893-6407
Fax: (408) 527-6351

petre@iaria.org

Additional copies of this publication are available from:

Curran Associates, Inc.
57 Morehouse Lane
Red Hook, NY 12571 USA
Phone: 845-758-0400
Fax: 845-758-2633
Email: curran@proceedings.com
Web: www.proceedings.com

Table of Contents

PATTERNS 2023

Forward

The Fifteenth International Conferences on Pervasive Patterns and Applications (PATTERNS 2023), held on June 26 - 30, 2023, continued a series of events targeting the application of advanced patterns, at-large. In addition to support for patterns and pattern processing, special categories of patterns covering ubiquity, software, security, communications, discovery and decision were considered. It is believed that patterns play an important role on cognition, automation, and service computation and orchestration areas. Antipatterns come as a normal output as needed lessons learned.

The conference had the following tracks:

- Patterns basics
- Patterns at work
- Discovery and decision patterns
- Medical and facial image patterns
- Tracking human patterns

Similar to the previous edition, this event attracted excellent contributions and active participation from all over the world. We were very pleased to receive top quality contributions.

We take here the opportunity to warmly thank all the members of the PATTERNS 2023 technical program committee, as well as the numerous reviewers. The creation of a high quality conference program would not have been possible without their involvement. We also kindly thank all the authors that dedicated much of their time and effort to contribute to PATTERNS 2023. We truly believe that, thanks to all these efforts, the final conference program consisted of top quality contributions.

Also, this event could not have been a reality without the support of many individuals, organizations and sponsors. We also gratefully thank the members of the PATTERNS 2023 organizing committee for their help in handling the logistics and for their work that made this professional meeting a success.

We hope PATTERNS 2023 was a successful international forum for the exchange of ideas and results between academia and industry and to promote further progress in the area of pervasive patterns and applications. We also hope that Barcelona provided a pleasant environment during the conference and everyone saved some time to enjoy this beautiful city.

PATTERNS 2023 Steering Committee

Herwig Manaert, University of Antwerp, Belgium
Wladyslaw Homenda, Warsaw University of Technology, Poland
Patrick Siarry, Université Paris-Est Créteil, France
Yuji Iwahori, Chubu University, Japan
Alexander Mirnig, University of Salzburg, Austria
George A. Papakostas, International Hellenic University – Kavala, Greece

PATTERNS 2023 Publicity Chair

José Miguel Jiménez, Universitat Politecnica de Valencia, Spain
Sandra Viciano Tudela, Universitat Politecnica de Valencia, Spain

PATTERNS 2023

Committee

PATTERNS 2023 Steering Committee

Herwig Manaert, University of Antwerp, Belgium
Wladyslaw Homenda, Warsaw University of Technology, Poland
Patrick Siarry, Université Paris-Est Créteil, France
Yuji Iwahori, Chubu University, Japan
Alexander Mirnig, University of Salzburg, Austria
George A. Papakostas, International Hellenic University – Kavala, Greece

PATTERNS 2023 Publicity Chair

José Miguel Jiménez, Universitat Politecnica de Valencia, Spain
Sandra Viciano Tudela, Universitat Politecnica de Valencia, Spain

PATTERNS 2023 Technical Program Committee

Andrea F. Abate, University of Salerno, Italy
Akshay Agarwal, IIIT Delhi, India
Carlos Alexandre Ferreira, INESC TEC, Portugal
Danilo Avola, Sapienza University of Rome, Italy
Johanna Barzen, University of Stuttgart, Germany
Frederik Simon Bäumer, Bielefeld University of Applied Sciences, Germany
Martin Beisel, University of Stuttgart, Germany
Nadjia Benblidia, Saad Dahlab University - Blida1, Algeria
Anna Berlino, Consultant in Tourism Sciences and Valorization of Cultural and Tourism Systems, Italy
Fatma Bouhlel, University of Sfax, Tunisia
Uwe Breitenbücher, IAAS - University of Stuttgart, Germany
Alceu S. Britto, Pontifical Catholic University of Paranã (PUCPR), Brazil
Jean-Christophe Burie, L3i laboratory | La Rochelle University, France
Simone Cammarasana, CNR-IMATI, Genova, Italy
David Cárdenas-Peña, Universidad Tecnológica de Pereira, Colombia
Bidyut B. Chaudhuri, Indian Statistical Institute, India
Sneha Chaudhari, AI Organization | LinkedIn, USA
Diego Collazos, Universidad Nacional de Colombia sede Manizales, Colombia
Sergio Cruces, University of Seville, Spain
Mohamed Daoudi, Institut Mines-Telecom / Telecom Lille, France
Jacqueline Daykin, King's College London, UK / Aberystwyth University, Wales & Mauritius
Moussa Diaf, Mouloud Mammeri University, Algeria
Chawki Djeddi, Université de Tébessa, Algeria
Ole Kristian Ekseth, NTNU & Eltorque, Norway

Agostino Poggi, University of Parma, Italy
Vinay Pondenkandath, University of Fribourg, Switzerland
Beatrice Portelli, University of Udine, Italy
Claudia Raibulet, University of Milano-Bicocca, Italy
Giuliana Ramella, CNR - National Research Council, Italy
Ali Reza Alaei, School of Business and Tourism, Australia
Theresa-Marie Rhyne, Independent Visualization Consultant, USA
Jamal Riffi, FSDM | USMBA,Fez, Morocco
Alessandro Rizzi, Università degli Studi di Milano, Italy
Gustavo Rossi, UNLP, Argentina
Sangita Roy, Thapar Institute of Engineering and Technology, India
Carsten Rudolph, Monash University, Australia
Muhammad Sarfraz, Kuwait University, Kuwait
Friedhelm Schwenker, Ulm University, Germany
Isabel Seruca, Portucalense University, Porto, Portugal
Abhishek Sharma, Rush University Medical Center, USA
Kaushik Das Sharma, University of Calcutta, India
Diksha Shukla, University of Wyoming, USA
Md. Maruf Hossain Shuvo, Khulna University of Engineering & Technology (KUET), Bangladesh
Patrick Siarry, Université Paris-Est Créteil, France
Marjana Prifti Skënduli, University of New York, Tirana, Albania
Jan Spoor, Karlsruhe Institute of Technology, Germany
Marek Suchánek, Czech Technical University in Prague, Czech Republic
Shanyu Tang, University of West London, UK
J. A. Tenreiro Machado, Polytechnic of Porto, Portugal
Jamal Toutouh, University of Malaga, Spain
Alexander Troussov, Russian Presidential Academy of National Economy and Public Administration (RANEPA), Russia
Hiroyasu Usami, Chubu University, Japan
Mario Vento, University of Salerno, Italy
Stella Vetova, Technical University of Sofia, Bulgaria
Panagiotis Vlamos, Ionian University, Greece
Sulaiman Khail Waheedullah, Slovak University of Technology in Bratislava, Czech Republic
Huiling Wang, Tampere University, Finland
Hazem Wannous, UniversityofLille | IMT Lille Douai, France
Jens Weber, Baden-Wuerttemberg Cooperative State University Loerrach, Germany
Beilei Xu, Rochester Data Science Consortium | University of Rochester, USA
Ziming Zhang, Worcester Polytechnic Institute, USA
Ester Zumpano, University of Calabria, Italy

Copyright Information

For your reference, this is the text governing the copyright release for material published by IARIA.

The copyright release is a transfer of publication rights, which allows IARIA and its partners to drive the dissemination of the published material. This allows IARIA to give articles increased visibility via distribution, inclusion in libraries, and arrangements for submission to indexes.

I, the undersigned, declare that the article is original, and that I represent the authors of this article in the copyright release matters. If this work has been done as work-for-hire, I have obtained all necessary clearances to execute a copyright release. I hereby irrevocably transfer exclusive copyright for this material to IARIA. I give IARIA permission or reproduce the work in any media format such as, but not limited to, print, digital, or electronic. I give IARIA permission to distribute the materials without restriction to any institutions or individuals. I give IARIA permission to submit the work for inclusion in article repositories as IARIA sees fit.

I, the undersigned, declare that to the best of my knowledge, the article is does not contain libelous or otherwise unlawful contents or invading the right of privacy or infringing on a proprietary right.

Following the copyright release, any circulated version of the article must bear the copyright notice and any header and footer information that IARIA applies to the published article.

IARIA grants royalty-free permission to the authors to disseminate the work, under the above provisions, for any academic, commercial, or industrial use. IARIA grants royalty-free permission to any individuals or institutions to make the article available electronically, online, or in print.

IARIA acknowledges that rights to any algorithm, process, procedure, apparatus, or articles of manufacture remain with the authors and their employers.

I, the undersigned, understand that IARIA will not be liable, in contract, tort (including, without limitation, negligence), pre-contract or other representations (other than fraudulent misrepresentations) or otherwise in connection with the publication of my work.

Exception to the above is made for work-for-hire performed while employed by the government. In that case, copyright to the material remains with the said government. The rightful owners (authors and government entity) grant unlimited and unrestricted permission to IARIA, IARIA's contractors, and IARIA's partners to further distribute the work.

Protecting Your Online Privacy: Insights on Digital Twins and Threat Detection

Sergej Schultenkämper
Bielefeld University of Applied Sciences and Arts
Bielefeld, Germany
sergej.schultenkaemper@hsbi.de

Frederik S. Bäumer
Bielefeld University of Applied Sciences and Arts
Bielefeld, Germany
frederik.baeumer@hsbi.de

***Abstract*—This paper presents considerations for the use of Digital Twins for protecting online privacy and detecting potential threats. While Digital Twins offer a promising approach to modeling individual vulnerability and identifying online threats, there are still significant challenges to be addressed. One of the primary challenges is the need for diverse and comprehensive training data, as Digital Twin instantiation relies heavily on machine learning algorithms. To address this issue, the authors describe two datasets for Digital Twin instantiation based on Computer Vision and Natural Language Processing techniques. In addition, the authors also examine the limitations of current approaches for creating Digital Twins and propose potential areas for future research. The main objective of this work is to provide insights and considerations for the use of Digital Twins in online privacy protection and threat detection.**

***Index Terms*—Digital Twin; Privacy; Social Networks**

I. Introduction

In recent years, the widespread use of the internet and social media has resulted in an explosion of personal data available online. While this has provided a multitude of opportunities for users to connect with others and share information, it has also created significant privacy risks. The practice of doxing, or the public release of personal information, is a particularly concerning example of how online privacy can be compromised [1]–[3]. Doxing can lead to harassment, stalking, and even physical harm [4]. As the amount of personal data available online continues to grow, the risk of doxing and other privacy threats also increases.

To address this issue, researchers have proposed the use of Digital Twins (DTs) as a way to model the vulnerability of individuals to privacy threats on the Web [5]. DTs are computer-based models that simulate or mirror the life of a physical entity or process and are commonly used in the manufacturing and aviation industries to monitor, control, and optimize the life cycle of real-world assets [6]. In the context of privacy threats on the web, a DT would represent a digital representation of a real person instantiated by information available online [5]. Essentially, existing methods and approaches can be used here since modeling knowledge and merging data points of an entity have been practiced on the Web for many years. However, one of the central challenges is to find, extract, and disambiguate the smallest particles of knowledge. Here, modern Artificial Intelligence (AI) methods are used that can evaluate image and text datasets. However, there aren't yet so many available training datasets in the domain of privacy that make it possible to train these models. Furthermore, the individual pieces of information that can be found and assigned to an entity, both individually and in combination with other information, are to be evaluated in terms of their influence on the privacy of users on the Web, in order to ultimately be able to derive from the mass of information when a risk exists and users need to be warned.

The ADRIAN research project explores the use of DTs to model the vulnerability of individuals to privacy threats on the web (see Figure 1). The aim of the project is to warn users about the resulting threats that can arise from combined data and highlight the potential of DTs in mitigating such threats. In this paper, we discuss the concept of DTs and how they can be instantiated using information available on the web. We also present two datasets used by us and discuss the methods used to instantiate the DTs. Our paper reflects the idea of using DTs to model the vulnerability of individuals to privacy threats and the potential for further research in this area.

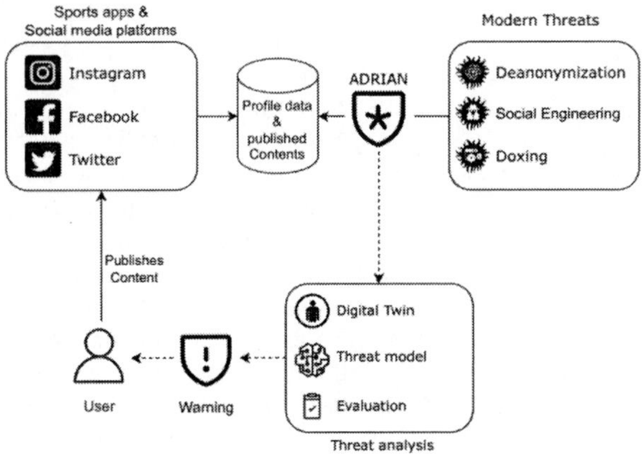

Fig. 1. ADRIAN Privacy Framework Overview

The paper is structured as follows: We discuss related work in the context of privacy research in Section II and describe our DT-based approach and datasets in Section III. Finally, we discuss our ideas in Section IV and draw our conclusions in Section V.

II. Related Work

In the following, we discuss the concept of DTs and show existing approaches for Information Extraction (IE) and modeling, both on text and image data.

A. Concepts for (Human) Digital Twin and Integration Levels

The term DT is an ambiguous concept found in various research and practice areas, such as mechanical engineering, medicine, and computer science [6]. Developments in AI have expanded its usage, with DTs defined as computer-based models that simulate, emulate, mirror, or '*twin*' the life of a physical entity, which may be an object, a process, a human, or a human-related feature [6]. DTs serve as living, intelligent, and evolving models that represent the virtual counterpart of a physical entity or process, used to monitor, control, and optimize their physical counterparts' life cycle.

There are three levels of integration for DTs [6]: (a) *Digital Model*, (b) *Digital Shadow* and (c) *Digital Twin*. A Digital Model is the basic representation of a physical object or system in the virtual world, without any automatic information flow between the virtual and physical worlds. Changes in the physical object must be manually updated in the digital model. A Digital Shadow takes this further and involves a unidirectional automatic information flow from the physical world to the virtual world. Sensors measure information from the physical model and transmit signals to the virtual model. A complete DT exists when the virtual and physical environments communicate bidirectionally, with information flowing automatically between both environments. This allows the DT to accurately reflect the current state and development of its physical counterpart.

With a look at sociotechnical systems, however, the matter becomes different. Sociotechnical systems encompass both human and machine components, making it relevant to explore the notion of a Human DT [7]. Despite its growing significance, there is no consensus on a standard definition or understanding of this concept [8]. The digital data that is available about individuals is often referred to under the term "*Digital Footprint*" or "*Digital Representation*" with the two terms often used interchangeably. These concepts are about data that is left by users on the Internet, often unknowingly and without clear identification or connection to the person. To differentiate the concepts of "*Digital Footprint*", "*Digital Shadow*", and "*Digital Twin*", several aspects can be considered, such as identifiability, active or passive data collection, individualized or aggregated evaluation, real-time or later analysis, decision-making authority, and comprehensive representation [7]. The Human DT aims to store and analyze relevant characteristic properties of an individual for a specific situation. This may include demographic or physiological data, competence or activity profiles, or health status [7].

In the ADRIAN research project, we understand the term as the digital representation of a real person, instantiated by information available on the Web [5]. In this context, the DT can never reflect the entire complexity of a real person, but it reproduces features that, alone or in combination with other attributes, can pose a threat to the real person. In this way, the DT makes it possible to model and measure the vulnerability of a person. The modeling of DTs is based on established and freely available standards of the semantic web, such as Schema.org and Friend of a Friend (FOAF). This makes it possible to easily connect and extend DTs. At the same time, the sheer number of possible sources of information, the quality of the data, and a multitude of contradictory data make modeling challenging. AI-driven methods from various fields, such as Natural Language Processing (NLP) and Computer Vision (CV), can help.

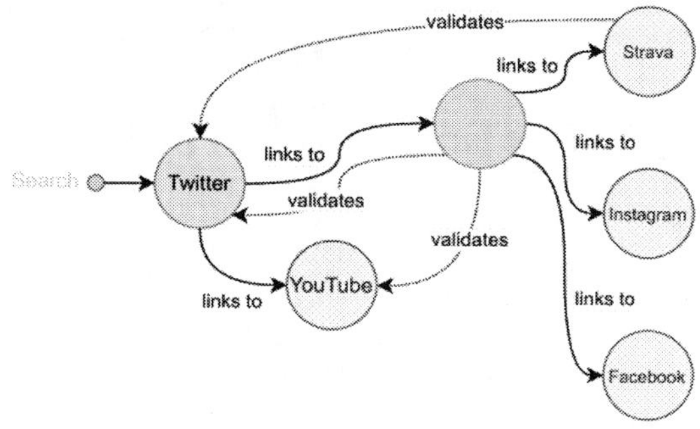

Fig. 2. Matching and Validation of User Profiles [9]

B. Instantiating Digital Twins using Semantic Techniques

Modeling DTs requires information that must be obtained from unstructured sources and heterogeneous datasets in the first step. In the second step, the information must be converted into a logical, semantic, and machine-readable structure. A key challenge is finding information about a person who can basically be on different social networks under different identities. Previous work in this area shows that interlinking between networks (see Figure 2) can be used in many cases to detect and verify matching profiles [9]. In addition, features, such as email addresses and usernames are reused (with variations) and, together with other features, enable profiles to be merged (e.g., profile pictures) [5].

For modeling DTs based on social network data, existing work on ontologies can be used. Different approaches have been devised to tackle the issue of interoperability by establishing shared standards for knowledge and information exchange. Numerous ontologies have been developed for the representation of personal networks, including FOAF and Semantically-Interlinked Online Communities (SIOC) [10], as well as for threats, exemplified by Structured Threat Information eXpression (STIX) [11]. Furthermore, Schema.org serves as an ontology for representing biographical information.

To extract data and map it into these structures (see Figure 3), different techniques are used depending on the type of data. Named Entity Recognition (NER) is essential for understanding and processing unstructured text data [12]. NER facilitates the identification and classification of specific entities like names, places, organizations, and dates found in unstructured text sources, such as social media content, web

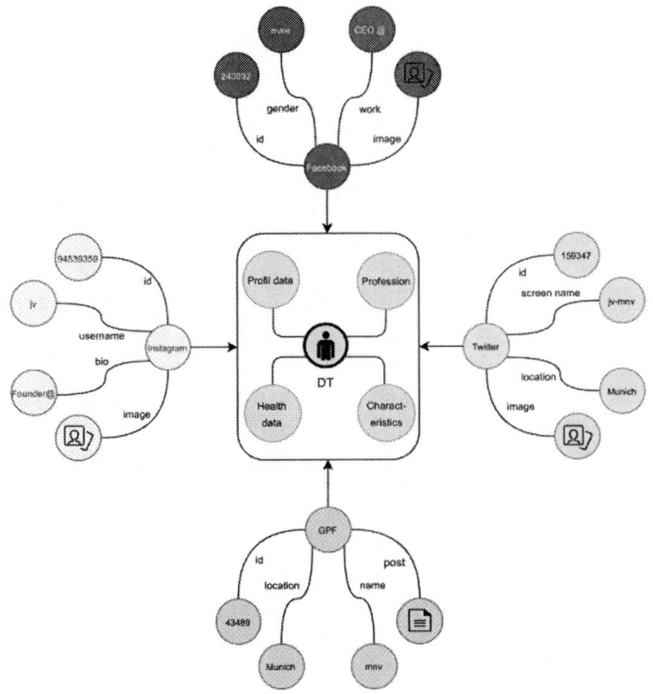

Fig. 3. Instantiated Human DT on Real Data

pages, and chat logs. However, the underlying NER models can be extended to recognize and extract different entities from diverse domains. Furthermore, recent work based on this also considers the connection between entities. One example is LUKE (Language Understanding with Knowledge-based Embeddings), which is a pre-trained contextualized representation model for words and entities based on a bidirectional transformer. It performs exceptionally well on various tasks related to entities, including relationship classification, where the model classifies the relationship between two entities.

Along with texts, images are a predominant type of data to handle. Models for understanding and processing visual information are currently being researched. Vision language models like Bootstrapping Language-Image Pre-training (BLIP) and Bootstrapping Language-Image Pre-training with frozen unimodal models (BLIP-2) have emerged for multimodal deep learning. These models are able to create representations between natural language text and visual input (e.g., images). This representation can be utilized for a wide range of tasks, including image captioning and visual question answering. Vision language models have the potential to enhance the analysis of images in the context of privacy and enrich DTs.

III. Enriching Digital Twins: Datasets

The two approaches to IE mentioned above are based on trained models whose training data do not necessarily consist of data relevant to the use case of this work. For this reason, models are fine-tuned to better fit the requirements of an application domain. In this section, we address two different

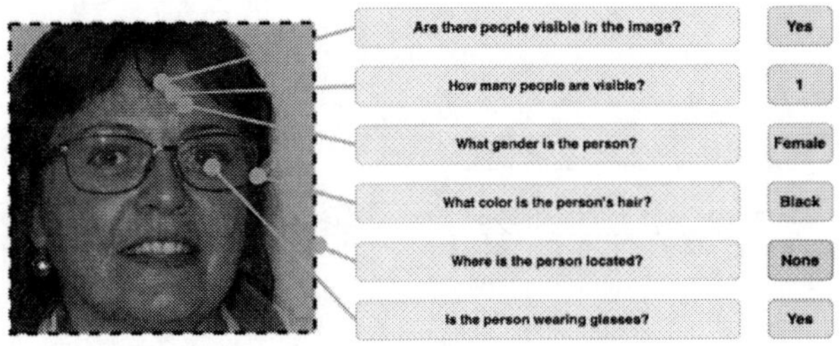

Fig. 4. Attribute Extraction via VQA

but related studies that examine the privacy implications of CV and NLP. In Section III-A, we discuss our work on developing a dataset based on the VISPR dataset [13], with a focus on human characteristics that may have privacy implications for visual content. In Section III-B, we explore the use of NER to identify potential privacy risks in German patient forums, particularly with respect to health-related entities from textual information.

A. VQA Evaluation Dataset

Extracting personal information attributes from images offers great potential to instantiate DTs. Especially on social networks, a lot of portrait photos are shared or photos of vacations (e.g., the Eiffel Tower in the background) and new acquisitions (e.g., cars). We develop methods that can extract and categorize this information. However, suitable evaluation datasets are lacking so far. In our recent work, we have developed a dataset based on the VISPR dataset [13]. The main goal was to extract sensitive information based on various human characteristics from visual content. The original VISPR dataset consists of 22,167 images with a total of 115,742 labels containing 68 personal information attributes. We focused on annotating a subset of these attributes that relate specifically to human characteristics (see Figure 4). Our dataset contains annotations for nine key attributes, as described in Table I.

These attributes include approximate age (*a1_age_approx*), gender (*a4_gender*), eye color (*a5_eye_color*), hair color (*a6_hair_color*), presence of tattoos (*a11_tattoo*), partial nudity (*a12_semi_nudity*), full nudity (*a13_full_nudity*), skin color (*a17_color*), and physical disabilities (*a39_disability_physical*). For each attribute, we specified certain characteristics to ensure the consistency of the dataset. Based on the dataset, we then investigated the effectiveness of a vision-language approach for pre-selecting relevant images and extracting human attributes as data enrichment in the ADRIAN research project. The BLIP model evaluated performed well in detecting the number of people in an image and in detecting certain human attributes, such as age, hair color, nudity, and tattoos. However, it had difficulty determining eye color and distinguishing between different degrees of nudity. Overall, the BLIP model performed well in human characteristic recognition, but showed weaknesses in document extraction.

TABLE I
FURTHER ANNOTATED VISPR CHARACTERISTICS

Attribute Id	Annotations	# Images
a1_age_approx	*child, adult, elderly*	1711
a4_gender	*male, female*	1863
a5_eye_color	*blue, green, gray, brown*	1348
a6_hair_color	*black, blond, brown, gray, red*	1759
a11_tattoo	*yes, no*	45
a12_semi_nudity	*yes, no*	247
a13_full_nudity	*yes, no*	11
a17_color	*black, brown, white*	1914
a39_disability_physical	*yes, no*	41

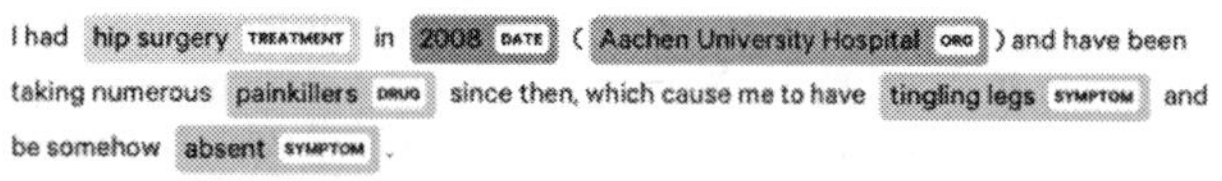

Fig. 5. Entity Recognition for Health Data

B. NER Evaluation Dataset

In another recent study, we evaluated different NER models on a dataset we created based on German patient forum texts. The annotated entities, examples of the entities, and the number of labels are shown in Table II. The focus was on the annotation of medical entities relevant to the instantiation of the DT, including "*Anatomy*", "*Diagnosis*", "*Diseases*", "*Drug*","*Symptoms*", and "*Treatment*" (see Figure 5).

The evaluated German BERT (GBERT) [14] and XLM-RoBERTa [15] models showed very good performance in accurately extracting health-related data from the texts with high precision and recall values. GBERT showed a better result for labels with a high number (*Anatomy*, *Diagnosis*, *Diseases*, and *Symptoms*), while XLM-RoBERTa showed better performance on entities with a low number of labels (*Drug* and *Treatment*). Based on these NER models, which can detect privacy-relevant entities in German patient forums, we are able to improve existing DTs. However, our approach primarily targets the recognition of entities in the text as the first stage of our research. Our plan is to extend this work by extracting relationships between these entities in the next phase. By incorporating relationship extraction capabilities, we will be able to identify connections, such as drug-dosage and drug-disease associations. This improvement increases the accuracy of IE and the quality of DTs in the health domain.

TABLE II
NER DATASET FROM GERMAN PATIENT FORUMS

Entity	Examples	# Labels
Anatomy	Eyes, Vessels, Intestine	1294
Diagnosis	ECG, Ultrasound, Gastroscopy	635
Diseases	Flu, Hemorrhoids, Stroke	3022
Drug	Omeprazol, Fluoxetine, Ibuprofen	390
Symptoms	Headache, Fever, Tired	1249
Treatment	Eyeglasses, Massage, Physiotherapy	361

IV. DISCUSSION

The use of DTs as a measure of user vulnerability to privacy threats on the web is an exciting and promising area of research. However, it is important to recognize the limitations of these models, particularly in the context of the complexity of the real-world entities they seek to represent.

One challenge in creating DTs is the need to accurately represent the vast amount of personal data available online. While tools and NLP techniques have improved significantly in recent years (see Section II), they are still limited in their ability to accurately extract and interpret information. Additionally, the use of standards, such as FOAF [16] and Schema.org for modeling DTs can help to improve interoperability, but it does not address the problem of the quality and consistency of the data. Moreover, the use of DTs raises concerns about the ethical and legal implications of the collection and use of personal data. As the amount of information available online continues to grow, the risk of privacy violations also increases. The use of a semantic web further exacerbates this issue, as the interconnectedness of data can lead to the unintentional disclosure of sensitive information [5].

In the context of the ADRIAN research project, it is important to note that while we aim to create DTs that accurately reflect the real-world entities they represent, it is *impossible* to create a complete DT. This is because the vast amount of data available online makes it impossible to monitor every piece of information related to an individual. Moreover, the data sources are very complex, for example, user-generated texts, which, with spelling errors, neologisms, and incompleteness, make IE considerably more difficult. Or images, which can be of very different nature and are also prone to leading to incorrect conclusions (e.g., a poster of the Eiffel Tower in the background as an indication of the location). However, this does not diminish the importance of our work. By combining relevant information from different sources, we can identify potential privacy threats and warn users before they become victims.

In this paper, we present the two datasets that we use to train and evaluate our AI-based methods. The VQA dataset can be used to evaluate further VQA privacy models, which showed very promising results in person characteristic recognition. A major challenge in our evaluations was distinguishing real people from statues, which requires further experimentation. As far as document identification is concerned, the model recognizes passports and credit cards but has difficulty identifying driver's licenses and national ID cards. The second dataset, based on German patient forums, was used to train and evaluate the German GBERT and XLM-RoBERTa models. These models show high accuracy in detecting medical entities. The distribution of entities in patient forums is very unbalanced. GBERT performed better on entities that occur more frequently, while XLM-RoBERTa performed better on entities that occur less frequently.

V. Conclusion

In this paper, we have explored the concept of DTs and their potential use in modeling the vulnerability of individuals to privacy threats on the web. We have demonstrated how DTs can be instantiated using information available on the web and the effectiveness of these models in identifying potential privacy threats. Our study highlights the need for increased awareness of the privacy risks associated with sharing personal information online and the potential for DTs to be used as a measure of user vulnerability.

While our study provides valuable insights into the potential of DTs in the context of online privacy, there is still much work to be done in this area. Further research is needed to explore the effectiveness of DTs in mitigating privacy threats, as well as to investigate the ethical and legal implications of their use. Additionally, the development of standardized methods for instantiating and evaluating DTs would be a valuable contribution to the field [5].

In conclusion, DTs have the potential to revolutionize the way we approach privacy threats on the web. By providing a measure of user vulnerability, these models could help individuals take proactive steps to protect their privacy and prevent doxing and other privacy violations. We look forward to further research in this field.

Acknowledgment

This research is funded by dtec.bw – Digitalization and Technology Research Center of the Bundeswehr. dtec.bw is funded by the European Union – NextGenerationEU.

References

[1] R. Jones, R. Kumar, B. Pang, and A. Tomkins, "'I know what you did last summer': query logs and user privacy," in *Proceedings of the sixteenth ACM conference on Conference on information and knowledge management - CIKM '07*. Lisbon, Portugal: ACM Press, 2007, pp. 909–913.

[2] A. T. McKenna, A. C. Gaudion, and J. L. Evans, "The Role of Satellites and Smart Devices: Data Surprises and Security, Privacy, and Regulatory Challenges," *Penn State Law Review*, vol. 123, no. 3, 2019.

[3] J. Pinchot and D. Cellante, "Privacy Concerns and Data Sharing Habits of Personal Fitness Information Collected via Activity Trackers," *Journal of Information Systems Applied Research*, vol. 14, no. 2, pp. 4–13, 2021.

[4] M. Chen, A. Cheung, and K. Chan, "Doxing: What Adolescents Look for and Their Intentions," *International Journal of Environmental Research and Public Health*, vol. 16, no. 2, Jan. 2019.

[5] F. S. Bäumer, S. Denisov, Y. Su Lee, and M. Geierhos, "Towards Authority-Dependent Risk Identification and Analysis in Online Networks," in *Proceedings of the IST-190 Research Symposium (RSY) on AI, ML and BD for Hybrid Military Operations (AI4HMO)*, A. Halimi and E. Ayday, Eds., oct 2021.

[6] B. R. Barricelli, E. Casiraghi, and D. Fogli, "A Survey on Digital Twin: Definitions, Characteristics, Applications, and Design Implications," *IEEE Access*, vol. 7, pp. 167 653–167 671, 2019.

[7] G. Engels, "Der digitale Fußabdruck, Schatten oder Zwilling von Maschinen und Menschen," *Gruppe. Interaktion. Organisation. Zeitschrift für Angewandte Organisationspsychologie (GIO)*, vol. 51, no. 3, pp. 363–370, aug 2020.

[8] K. Feher, "Digital identity and the online self: Footprint strategies – An exploratory and comparative research study," *Journal of Information Science*, vol. 47, no. 2, pp. 192–205, oct 2019.

[9] S. Denisov and F. S. Bäumer, "The Only Link You'll Ever Need: How Social Media Reference Landing Pages Speed Up Profile Matching," in *Information and Software Technologies*, A. Lopata, D. Gudonienė, and R. Butkienė, Eds. Cham: Springer International Publishing, 2022, pp. 136–147.

[10] J. Breslin, U. Bojars, A. Passant, S. Fernández, and S. Decker, "SIOC: Content Exchange and Semantic Interoperability Between Social Networks," in *W3C Workshop on the Future of Social Networking*, jan 2009, barcelona, Spain.

[11] OASIS Open, "STIXTM Version 2.1 OASIS Standard," jun 2021, https://docs.oasis-open.org/cti/stix/v2.1/cs01/stix-v2.1-cs01.pdf, retrieved 06/01/23.

[12] E. F. Tjong Kim Sang and F. De Meulder, "Introduction to the CoNLL-2003 Shared Task: Language-Independent Named Entity Recognition," in *Proc. of the Seventh Conf. on Natural Language Learning at HLT-NAACL 2003*, 2003, pp. 142–147.

[13] T. Orekondy, B. Schiele, and M. Fritz, "Towards a Visual Privacy Advisor: Understanding and predicting privacy risks in images," in *Proceedings of the IEEE International Conference on Computer Vision*, 2017, pp. 3686–3695.

[14] B. Chan, S. Schweter, and T. Möller, "German's Next Language Model," in *Proceedings of the 28th International Conference on Computational Linguistics*. Barcelona, Spain (Online): International Committee on Computational Linguistics, Dec. 2020, pp. 6788–6796.

[15] A. Conneau *et al.*, "Unsupervised Cross-lingual Representation Learning at Scale," in *Proc. of the 58th Annual Meeting of the ACL*. Online: ACL, Jul. 2020, pp. 8440–8451.

[16] N. Pankong, P. Somchai, and M. Buranarach, "A combined semantic social network analysis framework to integrate social media data," jul 2012, pp. 37–42.

Architecture Options to Orchestrate Digital Twins in an Industrial Metaverse for the Predictive Production with AI Methods

Evaluation of Options and Proposal for a High-Level Roadmap

Bernd Lüdemann-Ravit
Institute for Production and Informatics
University of Applied Sciences,
Kempten, Germany
e-mail: bernd.luedemann-ravit@hs-kempten.de

Frieder Heieck
Institute for Production and Informatics
University of Applied Sciences,
Kempten, Germany
e-mail: frieder.heieck@hs-kempten.de

Abstract— **The Industrial Metaverse (IM) is an upcoming topic for companies and offers new possibilities to digitalize and optimize their business processes together with AI capabilities. In the production domain, the Industrial Metaverse is a step towards the vision of predicting factory behavior for optimization purposes. A central challenge is a complete factory model necessary as the base to predict its behavior. Therefore, the IM approach is promising to build and contain this model out of available single Digital Twins of factory parts. Consequently, an IT target landscape is required to build an Industrial Metaverse for Digital Twins. This paper evaluates different design pattern options for an industrial IT architecture reference implementation of an IM that companies can use in current IT landscapes. It also proposes a high-level roadmap towards the proposed target IT architecture of an IM.**

Keywords-Industrial Metaverse; Digital Twin; Virtual Commissioning; PLC; Digital Factory.

I. Introduction

The term Metaverse is widely used at the moment to describe a virtual environment with the ability for immersive collaboration among participants using technologies such as virtual, mixed or augmented reality [1]. In the industrial context, a similar term emerged: the Industrial Metaverse (IM) [2]–[4]. In the context of manufacturing, the common understanding of this term is a virtual representation of a factory (Figure 1), either with a connection to a real factory as a Digital Twin (DT) of the complete factory, or as a model of the planned, not yet realized factory [5].

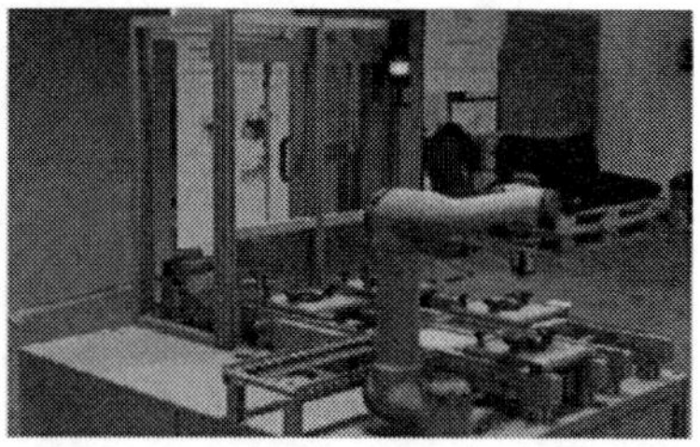

Figure 1. Example of a photorealistic Digital Twin in NVIDIA Omniverse

Several companies have started projects to gain the benefits of an IM, e.g., project iFactory by the BMW Group in NVIDIA Omniverse [6]. One of the most promising benefits lies in integrating Artificial Intelligence (AI) into IM. The vision is to predict the behavior of production processes inside a virtual representation of the plant so as to prevent unforeseen defects before commencing the real manufacturing process, e.g., path and action planning of Automated Guided Vehicles (AGVs) for intralogistics to avoid jams or deadlocks, or assembly of a rare product variant not previously validated.

After this introduction, this paper focus on use cases for an IM in Section II. Then, the requirements for these use cases are defined in Section III and related state of the art work is presented in Section IV. In Section V the single components of the architecture options are defined, The architecture options itself are presented in Section VI. This paper ends with the roadmap towards the recommended target architecture in Section VII and sums up central results in Section VIII.

II. Use Cases for an Industrial Metaverse

The following section describes use cases that it was not possible to realize in the past without an IM, or only with extraordinary effort. The listed use cases is not exhaustive, but it demonstrates the high potential that an IM offers.

Firstly, one of the most obvious use cases for an IM is to integrate planning data created by different production planning departments such as logistic, factory or process planning to check the validity, maturity and consistency of production planning scenarios along the product lifecycle [7]. Additionally, many external suppliers contribute to the realization of the factory. Therefore, a new milestone with an OEM approval for all suppliers based on the virtual representation of the complete factory, and not only parts of it than today, can increase overall efficiency of the realization process and boost reliability during the ramp-up phase.

Secondly, IM can be used as a training platform for employees to train processes or maintenance aspects before building the real factory.

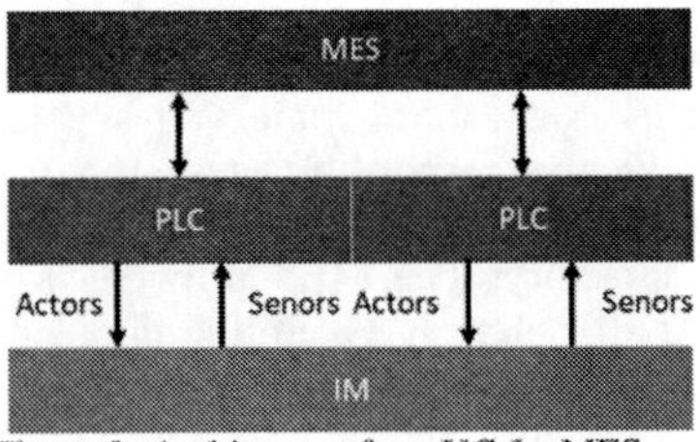

Figure 2: Architecture for a VC for MES

Thirdly, current virtual commissioning (VC) of single programmable logic controllers (PLC) is state of the art for original equipment manufacturers (OEM) in the automotive industry [8]. A VC of several PLCs or superimposed control systems, such as manufacturing execution systems (MES), is a new use case enabled by an IM (Figure 2) to validate control strategies deeply before ramp up.

Fourthly, the most promising use cases that an IM offers originate from its integrated AI capabilities to simulate, predict and optimize the production process before operation, e.g. to avoid undesirable incidents or identify optimized process parameters [9].

Last but not least, IM has an enormous potential to promote the use of AI technologies in real production scenarios in the factory by providing synthetic data to train AI algorithms to identify production problems, such as quality issues, using computer vision systems. In order to improve the accuracy and reliability of AI algorithms, the necessary training data can be generated out of the IM, whereas it is either impossible to obtain from reality or only very sparsely available.

III. Requirements

This section describes the main requirements for an IM used to predict production behavior.

A. *Integration into Business Processes*

First, the main requirement for successfully implementing IM use cases so as to achieve its benefits is its integration into the company's business processes. Figure 3 shows a proposal. This can mean either restructuring current business processes, e.g., integrating the VC results into an IM, or implementing new business processes, such as predictive production. Ignorance of integrating new technologies into business processes is a widespread pitfall [10].

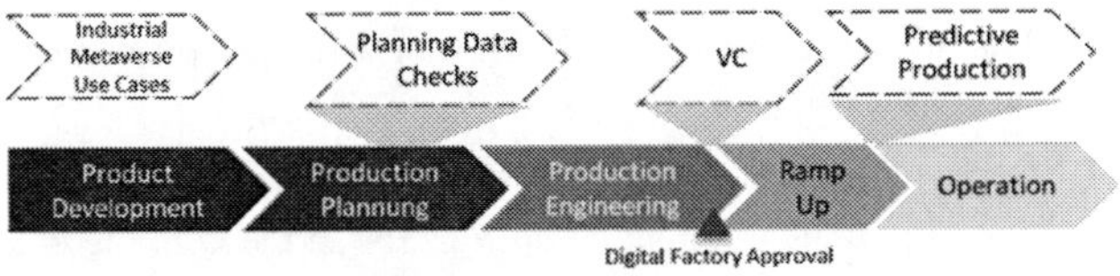

Figure 3: Use Case Integration into Business Processes throughout the Production Lifecyle

B. *Integrating IM into Current IT Landscapes*

The second essential requirement for successfully implementing an IM is its integration into the company's current IT landscape. Due to costs, complexity and time-constraints, a greenfield approach, that is the planning and realization of a complete new factory, is seldom practical. In the current IT landscape holding data for a DT of the factory, the following kinds of authoring systems can contribute to the virtual representation of the complete factory:

- Suites for product data management (PDM) and product lifecycle management (PLM) [11]
- Individual planning systems [12]
- Systems for virtual commissioning (VC) [8]

These IT systems need to provide some kind of interface to transfer data for the virtual representation of the factory into the IM. A new additional process besides the established business processes to build up this representation is generally not an economical solution.

IV. Related Work

DTs for VC to pre-program PLCs before the physical ramp-up of the controlled equipment have already been established for years in the automotive industry [8][13], especially in the body shop. In other areas, there is still a lot of work to be done towards extensively using DT for VC. DTs exist normally for single cells or stations, but there is currently no known VC system for an entire factory, as this would require VC of an MES. These single DTs are normally archived after the physical ramp-up, e.g., on a file system. If the automation equipment needs extending or reorganizing for new products or product variants, the DTs are reused to plan for these changes. In all other cases, the DTs are generally not touched after their physical counterparts have been built. The creation of DTs for a VC is performed using standard systems [8]. Current approaches add automated testing to VC systems [14].

Additionally, there are architecture recommendations for cyber-physical systems (CPS) to support a DT connected to its physical counterpart [15]. None of these are capable of realizing an IM where several people can collaborate on one virtual representation.

There are several architecture proposals for an IM, e.g., those cited in sources [16][17]. One of the most popular systems used in the industry is NVIDIA Omniverse (Figure 4) [18].

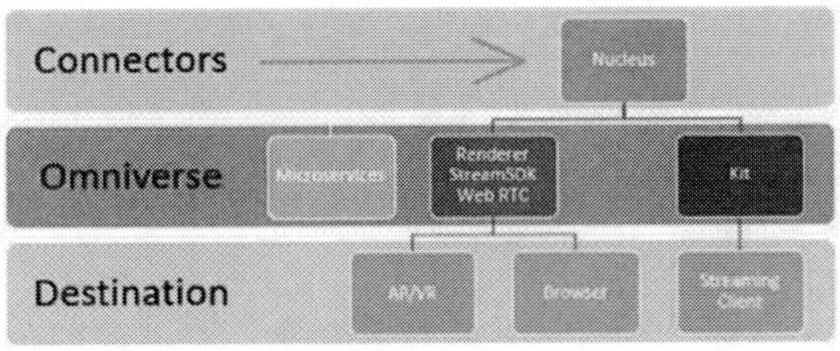

Figure 4: Architecture NVIDIA Omniverse

NVIDIA Omniverse (OV), which was released in 2019, is a collaboration platform for 3D production pipelines that enables multiple partners to work independently on different parts of the scene using a wide range of tools and syncing the changes instantly across all the tools. In order to facilitate this, the assets and scenes are represented using Pixar's Universal Scene Description (USD), as shown in Figure 5 [20], and accessed via OV's database and collaboration engine Omniverse Nucleus. Omniverse also supports material descriptions written in the Material Definition Language (MDL). Along with the developer framework, Omniverse Kit comes pre-packaged with a world-class rendering software and support for physics-based simulation.

The ability to connect existing authoring systems to the Nucleus through an open application programming interface (API) enables easy integration of existing IT systems into the IM. There are already several connectors on the market, e.g., for the VC system Visual Components or a proof-of-concept connector for the VC system CIROS. Through the API connector, a DT from a VC system can be streamed directly to the OV nucleus. The responsibility of the master DT can remain with the VC system. The standardized API connector makes it is possible for DTs created with different systems by multiple vendors to directly interact in a single virtual representation of the factory inside OV, so that there is no danger of a vendor lock between connected DTs.

Additionally, OV offers a large variety of AI algorithms that can be executed efficiently with high performance on NVIDIA hardware. These are ideal prerequisites for implementing AI methods for predictive production.

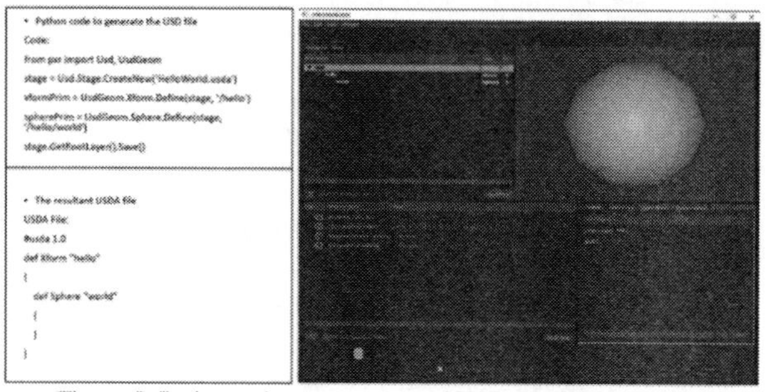

Figure 5: Python snippet to generated USD files and its rendering

Therefore, we focus our architecture options in the next sections on OV to integrate existing DTs into a single virtual representation of a complete factory.

V. Architecture Components

The following sections describe different architecture options for integrating interacting DTs into an Industrial Metaverse. Each architecture option orchestrates the same architecture components, as follows:

A. Programmable Logic Controller (PLC)

The PLC component interacts with actuators and sensors through a digital or analog input/output interface (I/O). The control logic that controls the sequence of the PLC outputs that are set according to the PLC inputs is implemented inside the PLC in a generally standardized PLC language [19].

B. Manufacturing Execution System (MES)

The MES is a control logic that superimposes current PLCs. The essential responsibility of an MES is to represent all orders, products, materials and other resources currently in use inside a factory. The MES provides Key Performance Indicators (KPI) such as Overall Equipment Effectiveness (OEE) to control the behavior of the factory. Modern MESs integrate functionality, such as the control logic for PLCs. The communication between an MES and the shop floor is also performed via digital/analog input/output.

C. Digital Twin (DT) for Virtual Commissioning (VC)

The information for single DTs of production equipment, such as a cell or a station, is stored in standard systems for VC [8]. These systems generally contain a geometric 3D model of the equipment. Additionally, the DT contains kinematic axis modeling to define the mechanical behavior of the linear or rotational axis of the equipment. Some systems support even the physics of rigid bodies, such as gravitation or friction. Besides this mechanical model, the objects have an I/O behavior model that communicates with the controller and other sensors/actuators via I/O. An example of a behavior model is a conveyor that starts with a digital input and informs of its current operation status through a digital output.

D. Industrial Metaverse (IM)

The IM is a platform holding the virtual 3D-representation of the factory. Additionally, it offers optional services such as AI, photorealistic rendering, or support for animation and simulation [18].

E. Orchestration Layer (OL)

The orchestration layer is responsible for synchronizing multiple single DTs, e.g., the overall sequence of processes in the factory. For example, the processes of DT B run after completion of the processes executed by DT A. Another example is synchronizing the flow of material between the single DTs, so that the virtual factory in the IM can manufacture a complete spectrum of digital products.

F. Automation Equipment (AE)

This architecture component represents the shop floor equipment that is controlled by a controller, either a PLC or an MES.

VI. Architecture Options

This section defines the design criteria and the architecture options of an IM.

A. Design Criteria

The presented architecture options for an IM with the goal of predicting production behavior differ in the following design criteria:

1) Location Control Logic: The control logic of the automation equipment is defined either entirely in the PLC, in a hybrid between PLC and MES, or only in MES.

2) Location DT: The services, e.g., the mechanical or I/O behavior model of the DTs, are located either in the original standard VC system or in the IM itself. VC systems are complex, and the current market leader started development ten to fifteen years ago. Therefore, a complete refactoring of the IT landscape for an integration of DTs into IM takes too long. It makes more sense to integrate available VC systems into to the architecture option.

3) Location Orchestration Layer: The OL is located either inside the IM or as an external component outside the IM. The main part of the OL is a messaging system to synchronize the multiple DTs. For instance, Kafka [20] , MQTT [21] or OPC UA Pub Sub [22] could be possible implementations. In addition, a protocol is also required inside the OL to define the semantics of the individual messages and the corresponding behavior of the interacting DTs.

These design criteria present the following six IM architecture options:

B. *IM Architecture Option A*

Regarding IM architecture option A., the DTs are located in the VC systems (Figure 7).

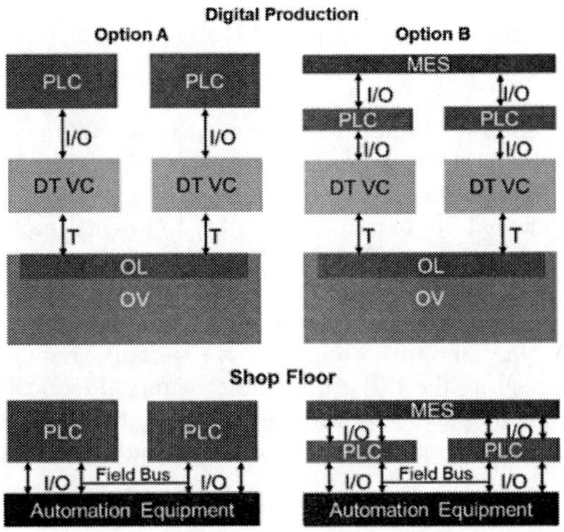

Figure 6: Architecture Options A and B

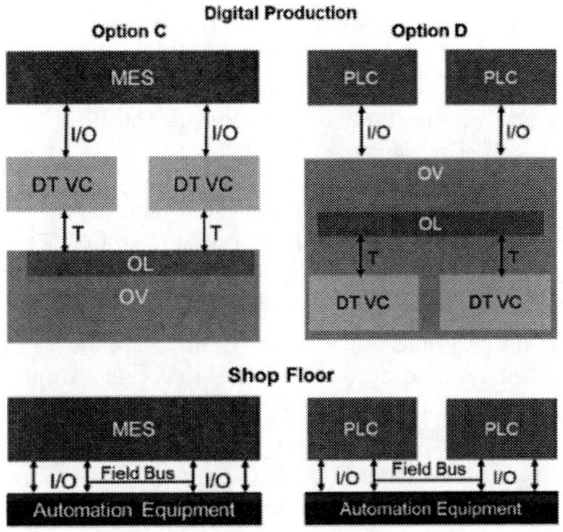

Figure 7: Architecture Options C and D

The Omniverse offers an open API, with which the static geometry of the DT is initially loaded from the VC system to OV through USD. The control logic is located in the PLC, as it is normally implemented on the shop floor. The PLC sends digital and analog output signals to the automation equipment inside the DT via an I/O interface between the PLC and the VC system. It receives digital and analog input signals from the DT about the conditions of the DT objects, such as, e.g., sensors. The VC system calculates the dynamic movements of the DT objects, e.g., linear or rotational axes. The corresponding changes of the objects' positions and orientations, defined, e.g., by a 4x4 transformation matrix T, are streamed from the VC system to OV through the API. OV does not calculate the object's trajectory in architecture option A. The orchestration of the multiple DTs in OV is implemented in the OL, within which the operation sequence and the material flow in OV are synchronized.

C. *IM Architecture Option B*

IM architecture option B (Figure 6) differs from option A in the way the control logic is implemented. Option A handles the entire control logic inside the PLC, whereas option B splits the control logic into two parts:

1) Control Logic in the MES: This part of the control logic handles the product variants or product orders, e.g., control logic for a specific product feature that other product variants do not have.

2) Control Logic in the PLC: This part handles control logic focusing on the shop floor, such as safety functions or real-time control logic for, e.g., axis.

D. *IM Architecture Option C*

IM architecture option C (Figure. 7) implements the complete control logic inside the MES. In comparison to option A, option C allows the implementation of control logic in one instance concerning multiple cells, lines or even an entire factory. This option offers much more flexibility to change the control logic in one instance than would be required in multiple PLCs in options A or B. The parts DT, VC and OV are the same as in options A and B.

E. IM Architecture Option D

The main difference in the IM architecture of option D (Figure 7) is the implementation of the DT in OV. In options A-C, the DTs were located outside the OV in multiple VC systems. As the features of OV increase, e.g., Omnigraph, it will become possible in the future to integrate the single DTs of the automation equipment into OV to create a single DT of the factory. Option D abandons all the VC systems because their functionality is integrated into OV. Despite the integration of the single DTs into OV, an OL is still required inside OV for the purpose of synchronization. An individual OL can also be implemented inside or outside the OV using the OV API.

F. IM Architecture Option E and Option F

Both IM architecture options E and option F (Figure 8) are addressed in this paper for the sake of completing the architecture options available with regard to combining design criteria.

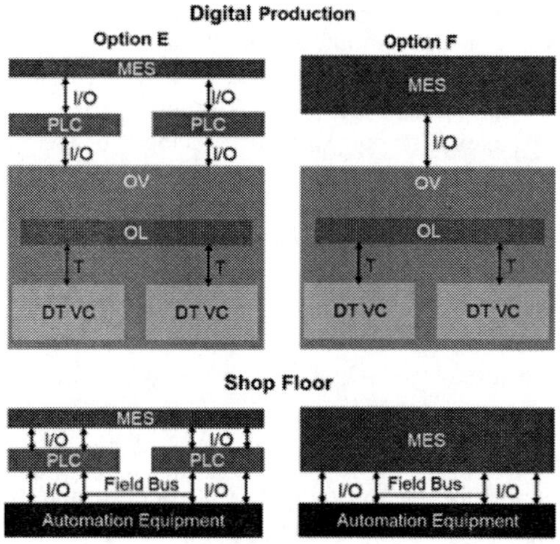

Figure 8: Architecture Options E and F

In options E and F, the DTs are implemented inside OV, similarly to option D. Also, the control logic of option E corresponds to the control logic of option B. Option F corresponds to option C with regard to the control logic.

G. Internal versus External Orchestration Layer

All diagramed options A-F show the OL inside OV. The advantage of an internal OL is the use OV internal functions to synchronize, e.g., the temporal sequence or the material flow among the DTs. The corresponding options A* to F* have an external OL with the same responsibility as their internal equivalents (Figure 9).

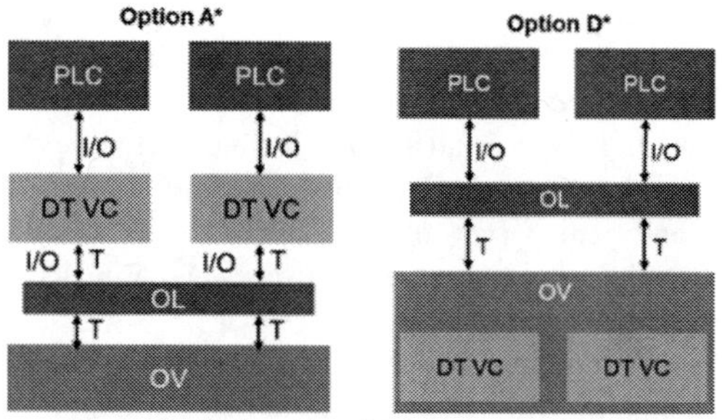

Figure 9: Option A* and D* with an external OL

With an external OL its tasks is getting more transparent. E.g., the OL of options A*-F* have to implement the I/O synchronization between the DTs to keep the transformations T of the 3D-objects correctly along the timeline. Additionally the OL has to know the ids of the DT objects to manage the transformations of the DT objects correctly.

The advantage of implementing an external OL is that it hides completely the OV from the above layers, e.g., the PLCs in option D* (Figure 9). Hence, an external OL offers the possibility to change the OV without a reimplementation of the OL and an adaption of the above layers.

VII. IM ARCHITECTURE ROADMAP

For simplification, we focus in this section on the internal OL options A-F, but the roadmap can easily transferred to the external OL options A*-F*.

Regarding IM architecture options A-F, one can find in most cases the implementation of the control logic as in option A or D, through the sole use of PLCs. The target architecture is implemented in option F with the following motivation: Firstly, because it offers the greatest flexibility in changing the control logic through its implementation in the MES system; secondly, the integration of the single DTs into OV offers the minimal number of systems required for implementing the DT of the entire factory. Practically, this reduces complexity concerning technical and organizational aspects and consequently license and maintenance costs.

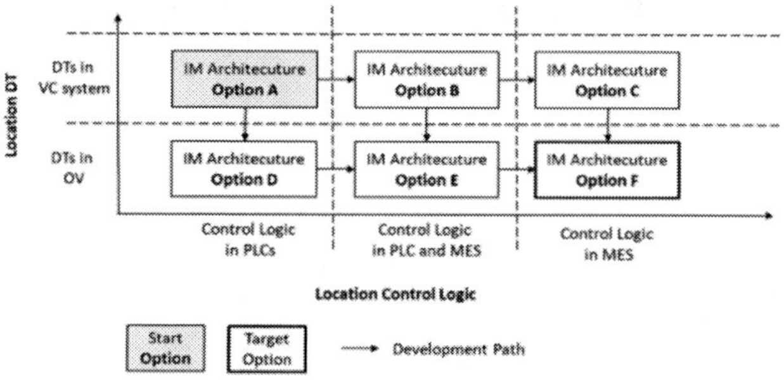

Figure 10: Roadmap for IM architecture

To implement an IM architecture, we propose a roadmap (Figure 10) starting with option A, because the regular control logic from the shop floor is not touched and the

existing VC systems need not to be replaced, but only an interface to OV to stream the positions of the DT objects. For the synchronization of the DTs, an implementation of the OL is necessary that can be reused almost completely with some adaptations in options B-F.
The roadmap assumes that with one development path, only one of the design criteria "control logic" or "location of DTs" is changed. At the current stage, there is no preferred development path. Its realization speed and costs is significantly dependent on the single roadmaps of the systems MES and OV, because MES will integrate today's PLC functions and OV will integrate present DT VC functions.

VIII. CONCLUSION

This paper presents for the first time different architecture options to realize an Industrial Metaverse based on the existing IT landscape. The two main assumptions are, firstly, that the existing control logic implementation found in current shop floors is based on PLCs, and, secondly, that to program these PLCs, current implementations of DTs for VC are based on separate VC systems within current IT landscapes. It was possible to define design criteria and to classify the architecture options into six categories.

Here, we have succeeded in defining a roadmap proposing a step-by-step implementation towards a target architecture. The presented architecture options are the prerequisite of the complete DT of the factory, which is the necessary to use OV internal AI algorithms to optimize and predict the behavior of production scenarios.

REFERENCES

[1] H. Pozniak, "Could engineers work in the metaverse?", *Engineering & Technology*, vol. 17, no.4, pp. 99–106, May 2022.

[2] J. Lee, P. Kundu, "Integrated cyber-physical systems and industrial metaverse for remote manufacturing", *Manufacturing Letters*, vol. 34, pp. 12–15, Oct. 2022.

[3] X. Yao et. al., "Enhancing wisdom manufacturing as industrial metaverse for industry and society 5.0", *Journal Intelligent Manufacturing*, Nov. 2022.

[4] Z. Zheng *et.al.*, "Industrial Metaverse: Connotation, Features, Technologies, Applications and Challenges", in *Methods and Applications for Modeling and Simulation of Complex Systems*, in Communications in Computer and Information Science, vol. 1712, Springer Nature Singapore, pp. 239–263. 2022.

[5] W. Kritzinger, M. Karner, G. Traar, J. Henjes, W. Sihn, "Digital Twin in manufacturing: A categorical literature review and classification", *IFAC-PapersOnLine*, vol. 51, no. 11, pp. 1016–1022, 2018.

[6] N. Kshetri, "The Economics of the Industrial Metaverse", *IT Prof.*, vol. 25, no. 1, pp. 84–88, Jan. 2023.

[7] Y. Jiang, O. Kaynak, H. Luo, M. Liu, S. Yin, "Industrial Metaverse: Solutions from a higher-dimensional world", Nov. 2022 (*preprint*).

[8] T. Lechler, E. Fischer, M. Metzner, A. Mayr, J. Franke, "Virtual Commissioning – Scientific review and exploratory use cases in advanced production systems", *Procedia CIRP*, vol. 81, pp. 1125–1130, 2019.

[9] Y. Chen, S. Huang, W. Gan, G. Huang, Y. Wu, "Federated Learning for Metaverse: A Survey", 2023.

[10] G. S. Day, P. J. H. Schoemaker, "Avoiding the Pitfalls of Emerging Technologies", *California Management Review*, vol. 42, no. 2, pp. 8–33, Jan. 2000

[11] J. Duda, S. Oleszek, K. Santarek, "Product Lifecycle Management (PLM) in the Context of Industry 4.0", in *Advances in Manufacturing III*, in Lecture Notes in Mechanical Engineering. Cham: Springer International Publishing, pp. 171–185, 2022.

[12] C. Lorch und B. Lüdemann-Ravit, "A new IT Architecture for the Digital Factory", 2nd International Stuttgart Conference on Automotive Production, Stuttgart, Nov. 2022 *(in press)*.

[13] S. Suss, A. Strahilov, C. Diedrich, "Behaviour simula-tion for virtual commissioning using co-simulation", in *IEEE 20th Conference on Emerging Technologies & Factory Automation (ETFA)*, Luxembourg: IEEE, pp. 1–8, Sep. 2015.

[14] P. Bartz, M. Decottignies, Y. Montagnol, K. Kouiss, F. P. Terra, C. L. D'Elia Machado, "Manufacturing machine virtual commissioning: Automated validation of the control software", in *IEEE International Conference on Electrical, Computer and Energy Technologies (ICECET)*, Cape Town, South Africa:, pp. 1–5, Dec. 2021

[15] S. K. Jagatheesaperumal M. Rahouti, "Building Digital Twins of Cyber Physical Systems With Metaverse for Industry 5.0 and Beyond", *IT Prof.*, vol. 24, pp. 34–40, Nov. 2022.

[16] M. A. I. Mozumder, M. M. Sheeraz, A. Athar, S. Aich, H.-C. Kim, "Overview: Technology Roadmap of the Future Trend of Metaverse based on IoT, Blockchain, AI Technique and Medical Domain Metaverse Activity", in *IEEE 24th International Conference on Advanced Communication Technology (ICACT)*, Pyeongchang, Korea, pp. 256–261, Feb. 2022

[17] H. Ning *et. al.* "A Survey on Metaverse: the State-of-the-art, Technologies, Applications and Challenges", 2021.

[18] *NVIDIA Omniverse - Designing, Optimizing and Operating the Factory of the Future*, (12. April 2021). [Online Video]. https://www.youtube.com/watch?v=6-DaWgg4zF8&t=24s

[19] M. Tiegelkamp, K. H. John, "SPS-Programmierung mit IEC 61131-3: Konzepte und Programmiersprachen, Anforderungen an Programmiersysteme, Entscheidungs-hilfen", Springer, Berlin, Germany, 2009.

[20] G. Shapira, T. Palino, R. Sivaram, K. Petty, "Kafka: the definitive guide: real-time data and stream processing at scale", Second Edition. Sebastopol, CA: O'Reilly, 2022.

[21] S. Quincozes, T. Emilio, J. Kazienko, „MQTT Protocol: Fundamentals, Tools and Future Directions", *IEEE Latin Am. Trans.*, vol. 17, no. 09, pp. 1439–1448, Sep. 2019

[22] J. Aro *u. a.*, "Praxishandbuch OPC UA: Grundlagen, Implementierung, Nachrüstung, Praxisbeispiele". Würzburg: Vogel Communications Group, Germany, 2020.

Requirements for the Application of Knowledge Graphs in Automotive Manufacturing

Jan Michael Spoor
Team Digital Factory Sindelfingen
Mercedes-Benz Group AG
Sindelfingen, Germany
jan_michael.spoor@mercedes-benz.com

Christian Graewe
Automotive Connected Customer Journey
NTT DATA Deutschland AG
Erfurt, Germany
christian.graewe@nttdata.com

Jens Weber
Mechanical Engineering Department
DHBW Lörrach
Lörrach, Germany
weberj@dhbw-loerrach.de

***Abstract*—The application of knowledge graphs drives in particular the development of Digital Twins. Thus, the creation of knowledge graphs becomes an important objective in automotive manufacturing. In the current literature, multiple requirements are given. In this paper, we conduct a categorization of these requirements. In addition, we evaluate expert interviews to enable a comparison of the requirements mentioned by practitioners with the requirements mentioned in the literature. While the industry experts agree with most challenges and requirements from the literature, some requirements differ. Most notably, real-time monitoring is not seen as a high priority by the practitioners. The application of predictive maintenance is seen as a subsequent application and not as a fundamental feature. Lastly, the integration of external partners such as suppliers is seen as controversial between the industry experts. This conducted evaluation provides a foundation to further develop use cases and implementation concepts in automotive manufacturing. In future work, we plan to add technical implementation requirements and conduct first use cases of knowledge graphs.**

***Index Terms*—Cyber-Physical Systems, Knowledge Based Systems, Production Engineering**

I. Introduction

Within the highly automated Body-In-White (BIW) assembly of the automotive industry, an improved representation, documentation, and production connectivity as well as planning knowledge are required to further drive the automation level. For this purpose, knowledge graphs are developed for manufacturing applications. A knowledge graph is defined by Ehrlinger and Wöß [1] as a system which acquires and integrates information into an ontology and applies a reasoning to derive new knowledge. In their review, Buchgeher et al. [2] list among others knowledge fusion, creation of Digital Twins (DT), automated process integration, and program generation as use cases for knowledge graphs. Thus, the development of knowledge graphs is an essential part of the development of DTs and as such highly relevant in the current development and implementation of DTs within the automotive industry, in particular the BIW assembly. In addition, Spoor et al. [3] highlight the importance of knowledge representation within the BIW assembly for inference procedures of fault detection.

In order to drive the development of DTs and to improve existing ontologies, Mercedes-Benz decided to run an evaluation of the requirements for the applications of knowledge graphs. Objective of the initiative is the discussion of applications, requirements, and future use cases of knowledge graphs with senior staff members and industry experts. Thus, the academic view of knowledge graphs is complemented by the view of industry experts. This enables a refinement of the requirements for an application in the BIW assembly line. The results of the conducted interviews and the comparison of the results with the academic point of view are presented in this paper.

In Section II, an overview of the current literature is provided and the requirements from the literature are grouped and categorized. In Section III, the methodology of the interview process is described. Subsequently, the results of the interviews are presented and contrasted with the requirements from the literature in Section IV. To summarize the paper and to provide a future outlook, a conclusion is given in Section V.

II. Literature Review

As structure for the requirements of knowledge graphs, we use the ISO/IEC 25010 criteria [4]. In particular, we use the quality model characteristics and add specific technical requirements of knowledge graphs in the automotive industry per category. The sub-characteristics of ISO/IEC 25010 still apply as evaluation criteria of the requirements but are not additionally discussed. The ISO/IEC 25010 criteria are discussed in the literature and considered to be useful for the evaluation of software architectures [5]. The derived requirements for knowledge graphs from the literature review and the respective ISO/IEC 25010 characteristics are summarized in Figure 1.

Functionality As first step of the application of knowledge graphs, a suitable data preprocessing is necessary. This includes a check for redundancy and preprocessing in order to counteract this since duplication is a rather common problem in knowledge graphs [6]. In addition, it is necessary to have comprehensive data validity checks and conduct an extensive *Data Cleansing* prior to the import and storage of data since Machine Learning (ML) and Artificial Intelligence (AI) require solid databases for the training. Thus, Josko et al. [7] propose a data defects ontology for knowledge graphs. Weikum [8] states that it is crucial to think judiciously about data source discovery and data quality assessment.

As second requirement, the overall *Relation Modeling* using an ontological model as well as a query engine to access this information is necessary. Ontologies are developed by,

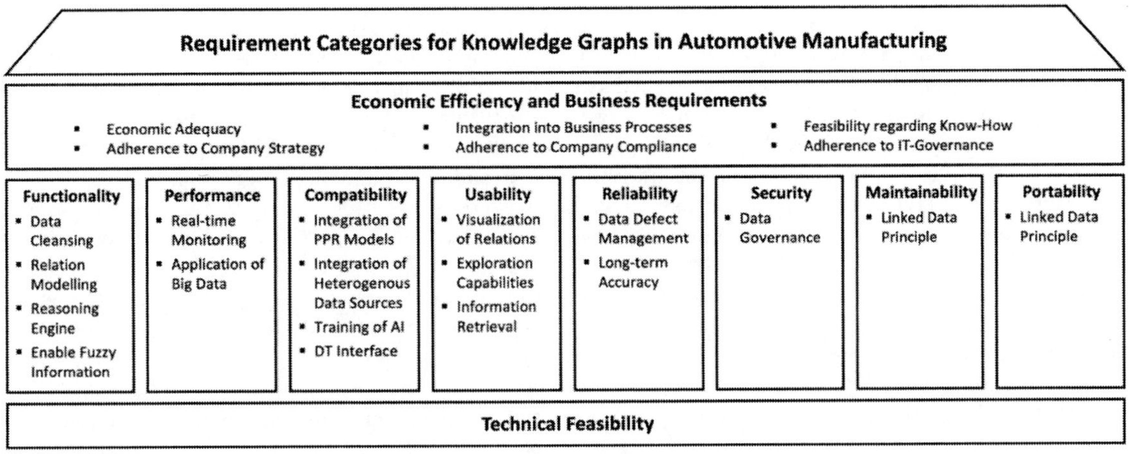

Fig. 1. Overview of the different requirement categories. Adapted from ISO/IEC 25010, we identified important requirements along the eight categories [4]. Business requirements are a cross-section to be taken into account in all vertical categories. All requirements rely on the technical feasibility of the concept.

e.g., Giustozzi et al. [9]. Most common in the automotive industry are product, process, and resource (PPR) models, e.g., by Ferrer et al. [10]. Yahya et al. [11] list as a requirement for ontologies that the scope should not be too application-specific and applicable in all areas of the production. Currently available semantic model-based ontologies are limited regarding this requirement.

Furthermore, the knowledge graph should provide an as-is-model as well as a defined to-be-model. Spoor et al. [3] see the knowledge graph as method for inference procedures and fault detection. Bellomarini et al. [12] differentiate a knowledge base management system from a knowledge graph management system since the latter includes Big Data and analytics capabilities. Ehrlinger and Wöß [1] describe the knowledge base and reasoning engine as components of a knowledge graph. Thus, the capabilities of the *Reasoning Engine* is a core functional requirement of knowledge graphs.

Since knowledge graphs most commonly use the Resource Description Framework (RDF) consisting of subject, predicate, and object, these relations have an uncertainty in case of inconsistencies within the applied datasets [13] and the data cleansing will not be able to resolve all inconsistent information. Thus, a knowledge graph should *Enable Fuzzy Information* and be applicable for fuzzy inferences. Noy et al. [14] state that each entity may have multiple types and specific types matter in different scenarios.

Performance Firstly, *Real-time Monitoring* and the speed of integration of new or changed data is a performance-specific requirement for knowledge graphs. In the literature, often a real-time data availability and processing is demanded [11].

Secondly, the integration and *Application of Big Data* is required [12]. Combined with real-time monitoring, this highly affects the ISO/IEC 25010 performance sub-characteristics of time behavior, resource utilization, and capacity.

Compatibility In this category, the main requirement is the *Integration of PPR Models* including existing, currently developed, and future ontologies. A knowledge graph should enable a problem-free integration of all systems related to the management of ontologies [11]. Different knowledge domains in manufacturing often use different systems and thus, an efficient integration of heterogeneous data from knowledge domains such as factory, building, system, resource, process, product, strategy, performance, and management is required [15]. This includes different applied systems within the production line, all relevant data management software applications, and also systems of external partners such as suppliers [16]. Thus, the knowledge graph has to be able to manage the *Integration of Heterogenous Data Sources* and extract knowledge from multiple structured and unstructured sources [14]. This results in interoperability requirements that are difficult to implement.

Knowledge graphs should in addition be able to provide data for the *Training of AI Models*. In particular, they improve explainability by applying the knowledge graph's reasoning capabilities [17] and function as fundamental source for the development of DTs by providing a direct *DT Interface* [2]. It should be noted that the boundary between knowledge graphs and DTs is rather blurred and implemented knowledge graphs themselves are sometimes considered as DTs [18]. However, knowledge graphs are most certainly important foundations for any DT development. Thus, there is a high relevance in the co-existence criteria between subsequent applications such as the DT or AI models and the knowledge graph.

Usability Within the context of scientific knowledge graphs, Auer et al. [19] name the development of methods for exploration, retrieval, and visualization of knowledge graph information as future challenges in the development of knowledge graphs. Thus, an appropriate *Visualization of Relations*, the *Exploration Capabilities* for finding new causal relations among the industrial data, and the possibility for an *Information Retrieval* of difficultly accessible knowledge are specific requirements. Although the original proposal is in the context of scientific knowledge graphs, these requirements are also relevant for the BIW assembly, the automotive industry, and manufacturing in general.

Reliability Data in real-world scenarios often lack reliability and thus, ontologies often contain errors, redundancies, inaccuracies, or contradicting relations in particular if different domain ontologies from different data sources are merged [8]. This results in a reduction of reliability of the applied knowledge graph. Thus, it is important to detect, identify, and mark potential reliability issues and inform users about these problems. Therefore, an applied knowledge graph must provide information about its own reliability and errors for users and industry experts to later correct these instances. Hence, a *Data Defect Management* for users to handle errors, redundancies, inaccuracies, or contradicting relations is a relevant feature of applied knowledge graphs.

A further aspect of the reliability of knowledge graphs is its *Long-term Accuracy* since the knowledge base continuously changes over time. Noy et al. [14] state that it is critical to manage changing schemas and type systems, without creating inconsistencies. In practical applications, a system needs to change organically based on changing input data due to, e.g., company mergers or splits, scientific discoveries, and organizational changes of divisions.

Security The ISO/IEC 25010 sub-characteristics are important for knowledge graph management systems. However, the application of a suitable *Data Governance* for the knowledge graph is most relevant as part of the overall IT Governance of the company [16]. This includes among others data security, data consistency for an improved decision making by users, profitable use of the data, and most notably an organizational concept for the accountability of the data quality [20]. Thus, applied knowledge graphs should also contain concepts for organizations and users to manage, improve, and correct data quality. This is related to the data cleansing and data defect management but differs since it focuses not on applications and systems themselves but the overall organization and company guidelines. In addition, this includes the organizational decision on the confidentiality of data and ontologies within a knowledge graph since malicious users could potentially use the exploration and information retrieval aspects of knowledge graphs to gain access to sensitive and business-relevant data.

Maintainability Regarding maintainability, the aspects of re-usability and modifiability can be improved by following the *Linked Data Principle* as stated by Yahya et al. [11] as an important future development task for improved knowledge graphs. These principles are as following: 1) the use of Uniform Resource Identifiers (URI) as names for entities, 2) the use of HTTP URIs, 3) the provision of useful information when searching a URI, using standards such as RDF or SPARQL, and 4) the inclusion of links to further URIs. The application of linked data is often difficult since the data owners are different organizations (or sub-organizations within a company), different URIs are used for the same real-world entity, complementary information exists across different datasets, the data is erroneous, out-of-date, or conflicting, and different conceptualizations of the domain for each dataset apply [21]. However, following the linked data principle enables a high maintainability and scalability.

Portability Using the same rationale as in the category of maintainability, the linked data principle also ensures an adaptability and replaceability of knowledge graphs within organizations. Thus, the linked data principle is a core requirement for maintainability as well as portability.

In addition to the requirements based on the ISO/IEC 25010 characteristics, overarching business and economic requirements have to be met within an application in automotive manufacturing. In general, the development, implementation, and use of a knowledge graph should follow economic adequacy. This includes development and running costs compared to the usage benefits such as among others reduced production costs, reduction of complexity, or faster production planning and development. This is realized by a prior development of a business case to ensure an economic cost and benefit consideration. Further, not only the technical implementation and integration into the IT systems but also the integration into the business processes must be considered. In addition, a company which wants to develop a knowledge graph should carefully consider their current know-how and availability of their IT workforce. If the development and maintenance of a knowledge graph cannot be conducted by current internal capacities, external capacities or an investment in internal capacities should be considered. Furthermore, the knowledge graph should be in adherence to the company's strategic direction, compliance guidelines, and IT governance. The business and economic requirements should be evaluated as a cross-section over the relevant vertical categories.

In conclusion, the technical feasibility of the proposed knowledge graph should also be evaluated since some requirements currently lack extensive use cases so that a feasibility assessment is not always completely possible. The technical feasibility should also cover the analysis of the current hardware and software of the IT landscape and the interoperability of these systems. Server capacities or applications of cloud or hybrid cloud solutions should be evaluated regarding available storage capacities, performance, and interfaces.

III. Methodology

Building on the developed categorization from the literature, guided and quantitative expert interviews were conducted. The methodology of the interview process can be structured into six consecutive phases. An overview of the six phases of the interview process is given in Figure 2.

The first phase of the used methodology is the development of the interview guideline and of a quantitative questionnaire. This includes questions regarding all identified special requirements. Within the guided expert interview the focus was the precise definition of the requirements from an industry perspective. Guided interviews were selected since they enable the interviewee to add necessary details and further ideas, concepts, or requirements not covered by the conducted literature review. The quantitative questionnaire was in addition designed to query the approval or rejection by the interviewee of individual sub-aspects. For all questions, the approval was measured using a five-level Likert scale.

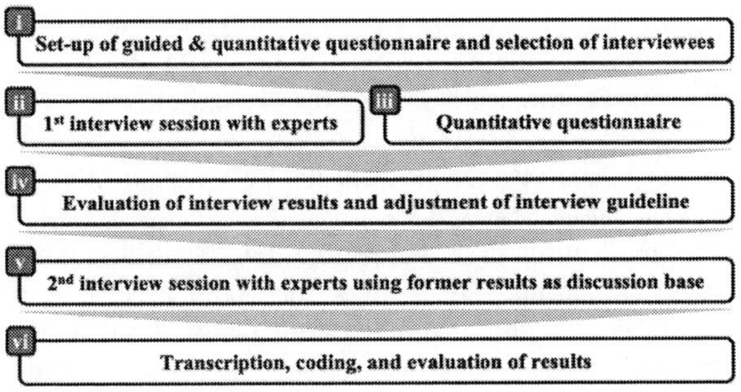

Fig. 2. Sketch of the applied methodology along six phases for the conduction of the interviews with industry experts from automotive manufacturing.

The first phase includes the selection of relevant industry experts. Only manufacturing industry experts with a high seniority levels of >10 years of industry expertise and either experience within data and knowledge modeling of the BIW assembly or prior experience with the development, application, or implementation of knowledge graphs were selected. This was checked via a pre-screening of potential interviewees and only interviews with relevant industry experts were conducted. Disadvantageously, this resulted in a rather small set of interviewed experts. In total, the whole described interview process was conducted with twelve industry experts (N=12) from German automotive BIW manufacturing departments.

After the first interview sessions were conducted, each expert completed a quantitative questionnaire. Subsequently, the results of the guided interviews and the quantitative questionnaire were aggregated to flesh-out relevant questions regarding the requirements and identify the most controversial opinions or opposing statements. Using the updated set of questions, a second round of guided interviews was conducted. In particular, the interviewees were confronted with statements from the literature or other interviewees contradicting their former assertions and asked to clarify their statements. Thus, the most relevant questions were discussed in greater detail and the assessment of requirements was further fleshed-out.

Concluding, the interview transcripts were evaluated using as coding categories the ISO/IEC 25010 characteristics and as sub-categories the derived requirements from the literature. We separated within the coding of the transcripts factual statements and opinion statements. After the first coding of the interviews, the requirement categories from the literature were adjusted so that literature and interview structure aligned along the new set-up requirements. These are the requirement categories listed in Section II. Subsequently, a second coding of the interview transcripts using the updated coding logic was conducted. The resulting statements were then analyzed, evaluated, and compared with the statements from the literature.

IV. Results

The results of the interviews are presented by descending order starting with the most mentioned categories. While this might not reflect the technical difficulties, it shows the focus within the practical application in the automotive industry.

The most mentioned and discussed category during the interviews was the *Integration of Heterogenous Data Sources*. The main concerns of the practitioners are the compatibility of different sources as well as the applications that access information of the knowledge graph. Applications which access the data from the knowledge graph are, e.g., Microsoft PowerBI and other analytics tools. Often, multiple analytics applications are in use within the same organization. Thus, multiple Application Programming Interfaces (API) are required for an integration within the IT landscape of the automotive industry. Important input data sources are the Internet of Things (IoT) applications and sensor data. A major challenge in particular is how to keep data within a knowledge graph up-to-date. The concern is often that the data sources need to be adapted prior to the implementation of the knowledge graph in association with a high level of necessary manual effort. Furthermore, data sources exist in different organizationally separated units within an enterprise such as production, maintenance, research & development, or sales, in particular aftersales. Thus, the German automotive industry sees the development of industry standards as a crucial part of a knowledge graph development. The integration of heterogenous data sources is discussed in the literature [16] and also a well-know current limitation and future challenge in the development of knowledge graphs [14]. Thus, the perception from the literature and by the industry experts match regarding this topic.

The next relevant topic is the applied *Data Governance*. Most interviewed industry experts and practitioners have referred to directives already in force within their company. Thus, the topic has already a high visibility within the German automotive industry. However, the details of the application are still part of a discussion. Multiple experts name data democratization, the idea of providing all employees with the necessary data, as a core principle for the management of the information generated by the knowledge graph. Other experts state that access control and access rights should strictly apply since a knowledge graph contains critical information. In addition, the access of suppliers, whose efficiency in providing solutions to businesses would be greatly improved as a result by the knowledge graph, is seen as a potential risk of losing internal company knowledge. Thus, the role of knowledge graphs needs further discussion within management science regarding the level of data democratization and integration of external partners and suppliers. While the literature states high benefits in the integration of external partners [16], this has yet not been sufficiently discussed in application.

Within the topic of *Relation Modeling*, the integration of contextual information and implicit knowledge by employees are perceived as important topics. While the context and implicit knowledge is perceived as highly relevant to understand the application, possible faults, and presented data, there is a lack of ideas on how to integrate the implicit knowledge and how to manage or update implicit knowledge. Since not all users share the same technical terms within large organizations such as German automotive companies, it is crucial to enable an identification of entities by multiple, sometimes ambiguous, terms. An exemplary case of ambiguous terms is the diversity of variants which are sometimes referred to as the same car model but in other instances strictly distinguished. Unfortunately, the embedding of implicit knowledge is considered necessary and knowledge graphs without this information might be of no value to users. Implicit knowledge is a well-know challenge in the literature [14].

Regarding *Data Cleansing*, there is a consensus among the experts that manual data correction processes are doomed to fail. The knowledge graph should provide functionality to automatically check redundancies, validate the logic of the RDF information of new or changed entities, check for currency of the data, and identify data defects. This is important since industrial process data and decision-making processes are highly susceptible to error and the current data sources are often inadequately prepared. This matches with the recognized challenges from the literature [8] and highlights the need to develop concepts for data validation.

The implementation of knowledge graphs according to the *Linked Data Principle* is very important to the experts and is discussed in the practical application. The usage of URI, RDF, and SPARQL is recognized by all experts as an important factor for the maintenance and modifiability of the system by software suppliers, as well as the connection with the supply chain. All experts promote a collaboration within the German manufacturing industry to align standards and ontologies. Projects within initiatives such as AutomationML are currently conducted and first results evaluated.

Regarding usability, *Information Retrieval* was mentioned the most. The idea to search multiple connected queries at once is seen as a core advantage of knowledge graphs compared to commonly used databases. Currently used databases are seen as opaque with a lot of unused data and as a hurdle to extract the necessary data. However, the experts are highly critical if the knowledge graph should display the full complexity to all users. The experts fear that users may not be able to find their way around and that too many functions and displayed data might be a hurdle regarding usability. Thus, the capabilities should be limited for certain users for an improved usability. This should encourage academics to further research and develop concepts in the field of user experience of knowledge graphs. The resulting transparency by a knowledge graph is seen as an important feature. This feature is enabled by user interfaces with refined information retrieval capabilities.

Most noteworthy, an application of *Real-time Monitoring* is seen as controversial among the industry experts. Although real-time capabilities are considered to be potentially useful, experts have doubts about the technical feasibility with the given IT infrastructure since currently implemented systems struggle regarding real-time data processing. Using a cost-benefit consideration, all interviewees list real-time monitoring as a subsequent, secondary, or optional requirement. This is in contrast to the literature such as Yahya et al. [11] and results mostly from the technical feasibility.

Similar to the information retrieval, the *Visualization of Relations* should only contain the most useful data and context information. Links to other entities should be displayed and the network visualized but the information should also be reduced to only the most relevant data for the given user type. However, the industry experts struggle to provide best practices and examples. Thus, it is concluded that data visualization is still a relevant future research topic.

The application of a *Reasoning Engine* is also not seen as highly important since other tools are already in place. The knowledge graph should be capable of adding more context to currently identified problems but not necessarily act as a separate reasoning engine. Thus, the knowledge graph as proposed by the industry experts is more similar to a knowledge base since Ehrlinger and Wöß [1] describe the reasoning as core differentiation between a knowledge base and a graph. Thus, practitioners see the knowledge graph as a method to add further context to already identified errors. The error detection is conducted in a separate application.

Regarding the *Integration of PPR Models*, the interviewees note that a knowledge graph should use current PPR models but PPR data are currently even within the same organization heterogenous and not aligned. Thus, it is important to merge, classify, and semantically enrich current models. One interviewee proposed to first build up a new narrow graph and steadily further develop and enlarge its knowledge base using additional PPR data. This is also acknowledged by the literature as a challenge and as a necessary requirement for the development of knowledge graphs [11].

The wide-scale application and *Training of AI* in production engineering is currently not achieved and seen as too far from a practical application in the automotive industry production. However, the knowledge graph is seen as a foundation of a useful database for future applications of AI and its explainability and thus, the necessary data quality and machine-readability should be ensured. More important is currently the *DT Interface* since the contextual information across multiple systems is an important success factor of the DT development.

An unsolved aspect is the *Long-term Accuracy* of a knowledge graph. An autonomous development and updating of the knowledge graph are seen as necessary but currently no solution for this topic exits. For example, if a part is changed, repaired, or updated during maintenance work, this should be noted and recorded accordingly within the knowledge graph. These updates of input data are frequent and thus, this processes must be automatically connected. Furthermore, with long-term use changes of the domain ontologies will occur and should trigger an automated update of the graph structure.

A second unsolved challenge is the *Data Defect Management*. It is unclear for the interviewees how problems in the database of the knowledge graphs should be managed. Proposals range from technically capable users as product owners, over rule-based consistency checks, to ML methods.

The interviewees see the necessity for an *Application of Big Data* since, e.g., an interviewee states that an exemplary manufacturing cell generates 37 GB data per day. Another expert states that a processing of 1 TB production data per day per factory location is currently feasible. As the amount of cells per factory goes into the hundreds, either data and features have to be selected prior or further Big Data capabilities must be implemented to provide additional functionality for large scale pattern detection and data mining. Solutions are in particular hybrid clouds where high-risk data is stored locally.

The industry experts are uncertain on how to *Enable Fuzzy Information* since some knowledge is not a priori known but predicted and fuzzy categorized. However, the knowledge graph should primarily display confirmed factual information. In addition, context might shift dynamically over time creating fuzzy transitions. Overall, the knowledge graph should act as a cross-section between predictions, assumptions, and facts.

The *Exploration Capabilities* were not a focus of the practitioners but the analytic deep-dive capabilities are recognized. The infrequent mentioning of this topic might be due to a focus on operation and not analytics aspects of most interviewees.

In conclusion, the economic benefits are named as cost reduction due to process optimization, improved product quality to ensure competitiveness, and an enabling of cross-functional and organizational collaboration on production data. Current IT governance and strategies are already in place to enable a development of knowledge graphs. However, internal competencies are still under development and communities within an organization are necessary for the education and training of employees in the application of knowledge graphs.

V. Conclusion and Future Work

This contribution lists the most relevant requirements for a knowledge graph implementation within the automotive industry and proposes a useful categorization for these requirements. In addition, the requirements from the body of literature and from industry experts are listed and compared.

While most requirements match between literature and practitioners, most notably, the real-time capabilities and reasoning engine are seen as a secondary priority since the knowledge graph should primarily enable users and subsequent applications to gain contextual information. In addition, the aspect of data governance and access rights for users and external partners such as suppliers are highly controversial. Thus, management science should focus on data governance concepts in the context of knowledge graphs in future research.

This manuscript is limited by the small amount of interviewed experts and due to the focus on the German automotive industry. In subsequent work, more international experts should be interviewed and their opinion compared to the here given results. In addition, we want to evaluate the technical requirements and implementation of knowledge graphs in the automotive industry in future research projects.

Acknowledgment

A special thanks to all interviewees for their time and the information provided. We also thank all colleagues and former colleagues who provided data, concepts, and development support of the research work within Mercedes-Benz Group AG and the University of Applied Sciences Zwickau.

Funding by Mercedes-Benz Group AG and NTT DATA Deutschland AG. All authors contributed equally.

References

[1] L. Ehrlinger and W. Wöß, "Towards a Definition of Knowledge Graphs," In: SEMANTiCS, vol. 48, pp. 1-4, 2016.
[2] G. Buchgeher, D. Gabauer, J. Martinez-Gil and L. Ehrlinger, "Knowledge Graphs in Manufacturing and Production: A Systematic Literature Review," In: IEEE Access, vol. 9, pp. 55537-55554, 2021.
[3] J.M. Spoor, J. Weber, S. Hagemann, F.S. Bäumer, "Concept of an Inference Procedure for Fault Detection in Production Planning," The Fourteenth International Conference on Pervasive Patterns and Applications (PATTERNS'22), Barcelona, pp. 10-17, 2022.
[4] ISO/IEC 25010, "Systems and software engineering: Systems and software Quality Requirements and Evaluation (SQuaRE)-System and software quality models," International Organization for Standardization, Geneva, 2011.
[5] M. Haoues, A. Sellami, H. Ben-Abdallah, L. Cheikhi, "A guideline for software architecture selection based on ISO 25010 quality related characteristics," In: Int. J. Syst. Assur. Eng. Manag., vol. 8, no. 2, pp. 886-909, 2017.
[6] M. Galkin, S. Auer, H. Kim and S. Scerri, "Integration Strategies for Enterprise Knowledge Graphs," 2016 IEEE Tenth International Conference on Semantic Computing (ICSC'16), Laguna Hills, pp. 242-245, 2016.
[7] J.M.B. Josko, L. Ehrlinger, and W. Wöß, "Towards a Knowledge Graph to Describe and Process Data Defects," The Eleventh International Conference on Advances in Databases, Knowledge, and Data Applications (DBKDA'19), Athens, pp. 57-60, 2019.
[8] G. Weikum, "Knowledge graphs 2021: A data odyssey," In: Proceedings of the VLDB Endowment, vol. 14, no. 12, pp. 3233-3238, 2021.
[9] F. Giustozzi, J. Saunier, and C. Zanni-Merk, "Context Modeling for Industry 4.0: an Ontology-Based Proposal," In: Procedia Computer Science, vol. 126, pp. 675-684, 2018.
[10] R.B. Ferrer, B. Achmad, D. Vera, A. Lobov, R. Harrison, and J.L. Martínez Lastra, "Product, process and resource model coupling for knowledge-driven assembly automation," In: Automatisierungstechnik, vol. 64, no. 3, pp. 231-243, 2016.
[11] M. Yahya, J. G. Breslin, and M.I. Ali, "Semantic Web and Knowledge Graphs for Industry 4.0," In: Appl. Sci. 2021, vol.11, article 5110, 2021.
[12] L. Bellomarini, G. Gottlob, A. Pieris, E. Sallinger, "Swift Logic for Big Data and Knowledge Graphs," In: Proceedings of the Twenty-Sixth International Joint Conference on Artificial Intelligence (IJCAI'17), pp. 2-10, 2017.
[13] G. Li, W. Li, H. Wang, "Querying Fuzzy RDF Knowledge Graphs Data," 2020 IEEE International Conference on Fuzzy Systems (FUZZ-IEEE), Glasgow, pp. 1-8, 2020.
[14] N. Noy, Y. Gao, A. Jain, A. Narayanan, A. Patterson, J. Taylor, "Industry-scale Knowledge Graphs: Lessons and Challenges: Five diverse technology companies show how it's done," Queue, vol. 17, no. 2, pp. 48-75, 2019.
[15] K. Agyapong-Kodua, C. Haraszkó, and I. Németh, "Recipe-based Integrated Semantic Product, Process, Resource (PPR) Digital Modelling Methodology," In: Procedia CIRP, vol. 17, pp. 112-117, 2014.
[16] M. Galkin, A. Auer, M.-E. Vidal, S. Scerri, "Enterprise Knowledge Graphs: A Semantic Approach for Knowledge Management in the Next Generation of Enterprise Information Systems," In: Proceedings of the 19th International Conference on Enterprise Information Systems (ICEIS'17), vol. 2, pp. 88-98, 2017.
[17] G. Futia, A. Vetrò, "On the Integration of Knowledge Graphs into Deep Learning Models for a More Comprehensible AI-Three Challenges for Future Research," In: Information, vol 11, no. 2, article 122, 2020.
[18] A. Banerjee, R. Dalal, S. Mittal, K.P. Joshi, "Generating Digital Twin Models using Knowledge Graphs for Industrial Production Lines," In: Proceedings of the 2017 ACM on Web Science Conference (WebSci'17), New York, pp. 425-430, 2017
[19] S. Auer, V. Kovtun, M. Prinz, A. Kasprzik, M. Stocker, M.E. Vidal, "Towards a Knowledge Graph for Science," In: Proceedings of the 8th International Conference on Web Intelligence, Mining and Semantics (WIMS'18), Novi Sad, pp. 1-6, 2018.
[20] M. Al-Ruithe, E. Benkhelifa, K.A. Hameed, "Systematic literature review of data governance and cloud data governance," In: Pers. Ubiquit. Comput., vol. 23, pp. 839-859, 2019.
[21] M. Mountantonakis, Y. Tzitzikas, "Large-scale Semantic Integration of Linked Data: A Survey," In: ACM Comput. Surv., vol. 52, no. 5, article 103, 2019.

Automatic Teeth Segmentation From Panoramic X-ray Images Using Deep Learning Models

Shuaa S. Alharbi
Department of Information Technology
College of Computer, Qassim University
Buraydah, Saudi Arabia
Email: shuaa.s.alharbi@qu.edu.sa

***Abstract*—A dentist's primary objective when screening for X-ray problems is to determine the shape, number, and position of teeth. Computational tools have been proposed to aid specialists in making more accurate diagnoses rather than relying solely on the trained eyes of dentists. Teeth segmentation and object detection are the core functions of these tools when applied to X-ray images. Segmenting and detecting the teeth in images is actually the first step in enabling other automatic processing methods. Medical image segmentation, especially in dentistry field, has been transformed by Deep Learning (DL) in recent years. U-Net with its different extensions and modifications has been among the most popular deep networks developed for medical image segmentation. However, it is difficult to determine which one will work best for teeth segmentation. In this study, different semantic segmentation models are selected based on their common use in medical image segmentation. Models include:U-Net++, ResU-Net++ and MultiResU-Net. Using panoramic X-ray dataset, MultiResUNet architecture performed better than the other segmentation models with an accuracy of 97.16%.**

Keywords: Convolutional Neural Networks, Deep learning, Deep Neural Networks, Image Segmentation, Medical Image Processing, Semantic Segmentation.

I. Introduction

Artificial Intelligence (AI) is becoming increasingly popular and widely used in medical care. The application of AI in the field of dentistry has shown successful results in the dental clinic examining routine [1]. Thus, AI can be used in dentistry to detect and recognize different variables from images, such as segmenting teeth from other tissues. Even though the use of artificial intelligence has grown rapidly and widely in the health care field, its application in dental care has been relatively slow [2].

In recent years, there has been increasing interest in applying the Deep Learning (DL) models for medical image analysis. The deep learning, typically the Convolutional Neural Network (CNN, or ConvNet) has made a significant contribution to the medical images analysing tasks especially the segmentation. Semantic segmentation methods based on DL have demonstrated state-of-the-art performance over the past few years. It has been demonstrated that these techniques have been successful in classifying, segmenting, and detecting medical images. For these applications, the U-Net [3] deep learning technique has become very popular. The U-Net shape with its variations and extensions (*i.e.* U-net++ [4], Resunet++ [5]) has long been recognized as the dominant deep network architecture. In this regard, it is the most widely used architecture in the medical imaging segmentation field.

In computer-assisted procedures topically aim to applied in dental clinics, teeth segmentation is an essential step. By using this technique, it is possible to provide approximate outline images of doubtful regions in order to provide features that can distinguish tooth tissues from other types of tissues.

In this paper, we demonstrate the use of U-net shapes to improve the performance of automatic teeth segmentation from panoramic radiographs. We evaluate the performance and segmentation accuracy of these model using a pre-request dataset provided by Intelligent Vision Research Lab (Ivisionlab) alongside its ground truth [6]. Based on the results presented in this paper, these methods can be used to improve the detection and segmentation of teeth in panoramic X-ray images.

The first section discusses automatic tooth detection in panoramic images. In the second section, the methodology for evaluating the U-net algorithm is explained. Three and four sections describe the results of the evaluation experiment and the setup, respectively. In the last section, the findings of this study are summarized.

II. Related Works

In the last two decades, teeth segmentation has been the subject of research, mainly using threshold, region-based methods and and machine learning methods.

Jader *et al.*, [7] present the development of the first method for segmenting and recognizing teeth from panoramic X-ray images using a region-based CNN (R-CNN). This algorithm adds a branch for automatic recognition of object masks simultaneously with the branch for class classification and bounding box recognition [8].

In order to segment the teeth from 3D dental model, Xu *et al.*, [9] proposes an approach based upon deep convolutional neural networks for segmenting 3D dental models. Further, Tian *et al.*, [10] introduced an automated method of segmenting and describing teeth from 3D dental images by utilizing OCTREE sparse voxel technology, CRF model based on conditional random fields, and a 3D CNN named OCN [11].

Furthermore, Zhu *et al.*, [12], studied the tooth segmentation and detection of teeth using Mask R-CNN. On the basis of 100 images collected from a hospital, their method successfully distinguished between complex, crowded tooth structures. A fully (R-CNN) method for automatic tooth segmentation is being evaluated by Lee *et al.*, [13] to evaluate it using individual annotations of panoramic radiographs.

A novel feature-steered graph CNN has been developed by Sun *et al.*, in their study [14]. Using this network, individual teeth were segmented and identified from digital dental castings. Towards this goal, the framework constrains its segmentation and labeling based on the distribution of crown shapes and concave contours. This method is more accurate than other DL-based dental segmentation methods, such as PointNet [15], OCTREE-based CNN [11], and the two-phase cast segmentation methods.

In Zhao *et al.*, [16], attention networks were utilized for the segmentation of attention in a two-stage network for localizing multiple teeth from a publicly available panoramic X-ray image dataset. Silva *et al.*, [17] introduced TSAS-Net for the segmentation and localization of teeth from the panning dataset.

Using comprehensive semantic data, Cui *et al.*, [18] presented a comprehensive method for segmenting teeth based on Generative Adversarial Networks (GAN's) [19]. This paper presents a deep segmentation network based on an automatic pixel-level tooth segmentation method (ToothPix) using a conditional GAN structure (CGAN). A comparison of the ToothPix method with existing methods, such as Mask R-CNN and Pix2pix showed that it outperformed state-of-the-art methods. Furthermore, as part of their efforts to exploit 3D cone beam computed tomography (CBCT) images that are robust to metal artifacts generated by the procedure, Chung *et al.*, [20] have proposed the use of CNN for pixel-wise labeling of CBCT images.

A U-shaped deep CNN (U-Net) architecture was used by Zheng *et al.*, [2]. The authors propose a variant of the Dense U-Net that is anatomically constrained during design [3] that is designed to integrate oral anatomy knowledge with data-driven Dense U-Nets. They aim to provide an automated means of segmenting and detecting lesions in CBCT images.

In addition, the technique proposed by Yang *et al.*, in their work [21] aim to combines mathematical analysis (*i.e.*level set) with deep learning CNN in order to segment the teeth from CBCT images. Where Leite *et al.*, [22] described a methodology for combining different CNN models to assess the ability of a new AI-based tool to detect and segment teeth from panoramic radiographs. They developed a detector that detects teeth and fine-tunes the segmentation map by combining DeepLab-v3 [23] architecture and a pretrained ResNet-101 [24] to detect teeth.

A novel technique described by Chandrashekar *et al.*, [25] combines independent tooth segmentation and identification models obtained from panoramic radiographs. Through the use of tooth segmentation and identification models, their collaboration aims to improve collaborative learning. Through collaboration, segmented teeth are identified and numbered to enhance results.

A recent study by Hou *et al.*, [26] described a Teeth U-net model for the segmentation of dental panoramic X-ray images. The aim was to solve the problem of accurate segmentation of all teeth in dental panoramic images and the determination of clear boundaries between roots. As a means of recovering image features in the network, dense skip connections between the encoder and decoder are proposed through the use of multi-level connections. Where Duman *et al.*, [27] used 434 anonymized, mixed-size panoramic radiography images over the age of 13 years as data, they developed automatic tooth segmentation models using a Pytorch implementation of the U-Net model.

In terms of teeth segmentation, the transfer learning models show promising results. Haghanifar *et al.*, [28] aimed to automate the process of segmenting teeth and detecting dental caries in panoramic images by utilizing automatic diagnosis systems. Through transfer learning, the proposed model extracts relevant features from x-rays and draws predictions using a capsule network.

III. Method

The dentist uses panoramic radiographs to obtain an overview of the entire mouth and jaw, including all the teeth, in dentistry. It has been used to detect larger concerns like infections, impacted teeth, and tumors. There is a low resolution in panoramic radiography X-ray images, which contributes to noise in the images. To process dental X-ray images, it is necessary to distinguish between the ROI and backgrounds [29]. In this research we compare 3 different CNN models that used regularly in medical image segmentation task and evaluate their results using a publicly available dataset. The following repositories contain all the code used in this paper:

- U-net++:
  https://github.com/MrGiovanni/UNetPlusPlus
- ResUNet++:
  https://github.com/DebeshJha/ResUNetPlusPlus
- MutiResU-Net:
  https://github.com/nibtehaz/MultiResUNet

A. Dataset and Ground Truth

It is noteworthy that panoramic X-ray images provide a greater degree of patient comfort than other radiographics, such as intraoral images (bitewing and periapical), and are less invasive, while examining a greater portion of the maxilla and mandible [30]. For dental image analysis, only a few datasets of panoramic X-ray images are publicly available.

Only a few sets of dental images were available for image analysis in the past, and almost all of these were intraoral X-rays (bitewing or periapical). The UFBA-UESC dental images dataset was published by Silva *et al.*, [17] to fill this gap, and it has proven to be a valuable resource for the community. The original data set was published with annotations for semantic segmentation only, which utilizes binary masks to distinguish teeth from non-teeth pixels. Jader *et al.*, [7] modified the UFBA-UESC Dental Images dataset to include instance segmentation information, and a total of 276 images

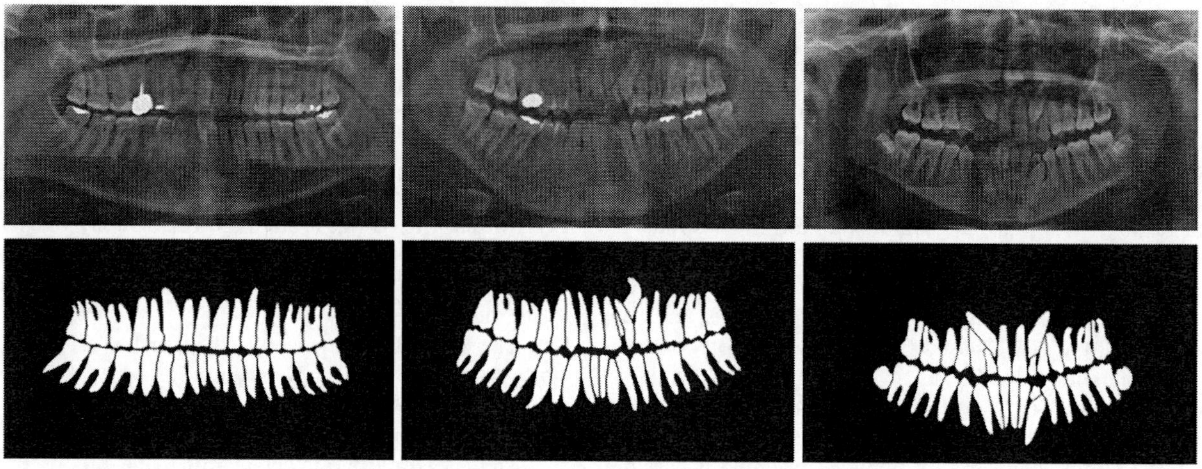

Figure 1: Three different simple panoramic X-ray images from Ivisionlab [6] alongside with their ground truth.

containing 32 teeth were used for training and validation, with the remaining 1224 images being used for testing. Recently, Silva *et al.,* [6] from Ivisionlab they annotated 543 images with number information (including the 276 used by Jader *et al.,* [7]) to evaluate semantic segmentation.

The dataset for this paper was obtained from Ivisionlab [6], [31] in order to perform our experiments . In this dataset, total of 1500 panoramic X-ray images with high variability have been grouped into ten categories in this dataset. It has also been updated with more instance annotations and includes information regarding numbering. A combination of panoramic X-ray images and ground truth images is included in this dataset. Figure 1 shows some samples of the dataset alongside ground truth.

B. Models Architectures Overview

1) U-net++ Architecture: The U-net++ architecture [4] in terms of medical image segmentation, is a more powerful architecture. There are several nested, dense skip pathways connecting the encoder and decoder sub-networks in this architecture. As a result of the redesign of the skip pathways, the semantic gap between the feature maps of the encoder and decoder sub-networks is reduced.

2) ResUNet++ Architecture: The ResUNet++ Architecture [5] is based on the Deep Residual U-Net (ResUNet) [32], which is a deep residual learning concept combined with an U-Net. There are three encoder blocks and three decoder blocks comprised of the ResUNet++ architecture. An encoder block comprises two successive convolutional blocks of 3×3 and an identity mapping. Using residual blocks, a deeper neural network that can solve the degradation problem in each encoder using residual blocks that propagate information over layers. Consequently, channel interdependencies are improved while computational costs are reduced.

3) MutiResU-Net Architecture: In MutiResU-Net architecture [33], a MultiRes block is proposed as a replacement for two convolutional layers. The number of filters in the convolutional layers is controlled by a parameter within each MultiRes block. A MultiRes block has been proposed in order to enhance U-Net's capability to analyze and assess data at multiple resolutions. In some cases, there is a discrepancy between the features propagated through the encoder network and the features propagated through the decoder network. In order to balance these two incompatible feature sets, MutiResU-Net offers some additional processing (*i.e.*Res paths).

IV. Results and Discussion

A. Evaluation and Assessment Metrics

In order to evaluate the predictive performance of each detection model, we use F1 and F2 scores. F1 scores are calculated by combining precision and recall, and therefore provide a more accurate measure of predictive performance than simply the percentage of correct predictions. Where F2 is defined as the weighted average mean of precision and recall (given a threshold value). A F2 score places more emphasis on recall than precision, in contrast with the F1 score, in which precision and recall are equally weighted.

A measurement of accuracy is used to determine how closely a measurement is to a standard or known value. Moreover, segmentation tasks are commonly evaluated by Dice scores and Jaccard indices in medical imaging. It is common for convolutional neural networks to be optimized for cross-entropy (weighted) when they are trained to segment images. The purpose of this measurment is essentially to quantify the overlap between our prediction output and the target mask.

The relevant mathematical expressions are as follows:

$$\text{Precision} = \frac{TP}{TP + FP} \tag{1}$$

$$\text{Recall (Sensitivity)} = \frac{TN}{TN + FP} \tag{2}$$

$$\text{F1-Measure} = \frac{2 \cdot TP}{2 \cdot TP + FP + FN} \tag{3}$$

$$\text{F2-Measure} = \frac{TP}{TP + 0.2 \cdot 0.8FN} \quad (4)$$

$$\text{Accuracy} = \frac{TP + TN}{TP + TN + FP + FN} \quad (5)$$

$$\text{Jaccard index} = \frac{TP}{TP + FN + FP} \quad (6)$$

Where TP is true positive, TN—true negative, FP—false positive, and FN—false negative cases.

B. Quantitative and Qualitative Comparison

In the following Table I and Figure 2, U-Net shape CNN models are quantitatively analyzed using IvisionLab data [6]. It is notable that MutiResU-Net outperformed compare with other methods with accuracy of 97.16%. This is because MutiResU-Net performs better on heterogeneous datasets than classical U-Net [33].

V. Experiments

The experiments were conducted using Python, more specifically Python3 [34]. Where in order to construct the network models, Keras [35] was used with Tensorflow [36] as the backend.

VI. Conclusion

The results of our study indicate that MutiResU-Net may succeed the other U-Net architectures in the future, particularly when it comes to segmenting teeth from panoramic X-ray images. This experiment and assumption relied on a single dataset for the evaluation of different models, which could explain why MultiResU-Net performed better. Future research should conduct experiments with different datasets to see whether this claim holds.

Acknowledgment

The author extend her appreciation to the Deputyship for Research& Innovation, Ministry of Education, and Qassim University, Saudi Arabia, for funding this research work. The author also thank to Qassim University for technical support.

References

[1] D. L. Duong, M. H. Kabir, and R. F. Kuo, "Automated caries detection with smartphone color photography using machine learning," *Health Informatics Journal*, vol. 27, no. 2, p. 14604582211007530, 2021.

[2] Z. Zheng, H. Yan, F. C. Setzer, K. J. Shi, M. Mupparapu, and J. Li, "Anatomically constrained deep learning for automating dental cbct segmentation and lesion detection," *IEEE Transactions on Automation Science and Engineering*, vol. 18, no. 2, pp. 603–614, 2020.

[3] O. Ronneberger, P. Fischer, and T. Brox, "U-net: Convolutional networks for biomedical image segmentation," in *International Conference on Medical image computing and computer-assisted intervention*. Springer, 2015, pp. 234–241.

[4] Z. Zhou, M. M. Rahman Siddiquee, N. Tajbakhsh, and J. Liang, "Unet++: A nested u-net architecture for medical image segmentation," in *Deep Learning in Medical Image Analysis and Multimodal Learning for Clinical Decision Support: International Workshop, DLMIA 2018, and 8th International Workshop, ML-CDS 2018, Held in Conjunction with MICCAI 2018, Granada, Spain, September 20, 2018, Proceedings 4*, 2018, pp. 3–11.

[5] D. Jha, P. H. Smedsrud, M. A. Riegler, D. Johansen, T. De Lange, P. Halvorsen, and H. D. Johansen, "Resunet++: An advanced architecture for medical image segmentation," in *2019 IEEE International Symposium on Multimedia (ISM)*, 2019, pp. 225–2255.

[6] B. Silva, L. Pinheiro, L. Oliveira, and M. Pithon, "A study on tooth segmentation and numbering using end-to-end deep neural networks," in *Conference on Graphics, Patterns and Images (SIBGRAPI)*, 2020, pp. 164–171.

[7] G. Jader, J. Fontineli, M. Ruiz, K. Abdalla, M. Pithon, and L. Oliveira, "Deep instance segmentation of teeth in panoramic x-ray images," in *Conference on Graphics, Patterns and Images (SIBGRAPI)*, 2018, pp. 400–407.

[8] K. He, G. Gkioxari, P. Dollár, and R. Girshick, "Mask r-cnn," in *Proceedings of the IEEE international conference on computer vision*, 2017, pp. 2961–2969.

[9] X. Xu, C. Liu, and Y. Zheng, "3d tooth segmentation and labeling using deep convolutional neural networks," *IEEE transactions on visualization and computer graphics*, vol. 25, no. 7, pp. 2336–2348, 2018.

[10] S. Tian, N. Dai, B. Zhang, F. Yuan, Q. Yu, and X. Cheng, "Automatic classification and segmentation of teeth on 3d dental model using hierarchical deep learning networks," *IEEE Access*, vol. 7, pp. 84 817–84 828, 2019.

[11] P.-S. Wang, Y. Liu, Y.-X. Guo, C.-Y. Sun, and X. Tong, "O-cnn: Octree-based convolutional neural networks for 3d shape analysis," *ACM Transactions On Graphics (TOG)*, vol. 36, no. 4, pp. 1–11, 2017.

[12] G. Zhu, Z. Piao, and S. C. Kim, "Tooth detection and segmentation with mask r-cnn," in *2020 International Conference on Artificial Intelligence in Information and Communication (ICAIIC)*, 2020, pp. 070–072.

[13] J.-H. Lee, S.-S. Han, Y. H. Kim, C. Lee, and I. Kim, "Application of a fully deep convolutional neural network to the automation of tooth segmentation on panoramic radiographs," *Oral Surgery, Oral Medicine, Oral Pathology and Oral Radiology*, vol. 129, no. 6, pp. 635–642, 2020.

[14] D. Sun, Y. Pei, G. Song, Y. Guo, G. Ma, T. Xu, and H. Zha, "Tooth segmentation and labeling from digital dental casts," in *2020 IEEE 17th International Symposium on Biomedical Imaging (ISBI)*, 2020, pp. 669–673.

[15] C. R. Qi, H. Su, K. Mo, and L. J. Guibas, "Pointnet: Deep learning on point sets for 3d classification and segmentation," in *Proceedings of the IEEE conference on computer vision and pattern recognition*, 2017, pp. 652–660.

[16] Y. Zhao, P. Li, C. Gao, Y. Liu, Q. Chen, F. Yang, and D. Meng, "Tsasnet: Tooth segmentation on dental panoramic x-ray images by two-stage attention segmentation network," *Knowledge-Based Systems*, vol. 206, p. 106338, 2020.

[17] G. Silva, L. Oliveira, and M. Pithon, "Automatic segmenting teeth in x-ray images: Trends, a novel data set, benchmarking and future perspectives," *Expert Systems with Applications*, vol. 107, pp. 15–31, 2018.

[18] W. Cui, L. Zeng, B. Chong, and Q. Zhang, "Toothpix: Pixel-level tooth segmentation in panoramic x-ray images based on generative adversarial networks," in *International Symposium on Biomedical Imaging (ISBI)*, 2021, pp. 1346–1350.

[19] M.-Y. Liu and O. Tuzel, "Coupled generative adversarial networks," *Advances in Neural Information Processing Systems*, vol. 29, 2016.

[20] M. Chung, M. Lee, J. Hong, S. Park, J. Lee, J. Lee, I.-H. Yang, J. Lee, and Y.-G. Shin, "Pose-aware instance segmentation framework from cone beam ct images for tooth segmentation," *Computers in biology and medicine*, vol. 120, p. 103720, 2020.

[21] Y. Yang, R. Xie, W. Jia, Z. Chen, Y. Yang, L. Xie, and B. Jiang, "Accurate and automatic tooth image segmentation model with deep convolutional neural networks and level set method," *Neurocomputing*, vol. 419, pp. 108–125, 2021.

[22] A. F. Leite, A. V. Gerven, H. Willems, T. Beznik, P. Lahoud, H. Gaêta-Araujo, M. Vranckx, and R. Jacobs, "Artificial intelligence-driven novel tool for tooth detection and segmentation on panoramic radiographs," *Clinical oral investigations*, vol. 25, no. 4, pp. 2257–2267, 2021.

[23] L.-C. Chen, G. Papandreou, F. Schroff, and H. Adam, "Rethinking atrous convolution for semantic image segmentation," *arXiv preprint arXiv:1706.05587*, 2017.

[24] Y. Rao, L. He, and J. Zhu, "A residual convolutional neural network for pan-shaprening," in *2017 International Workshop on Remote Sensing with Intelligent Processing (RSIP)*. IEEE, 2017, pp. 1–4.

[25] G. Chandrashekar, S. AlQarni, E. E. Bumann, and Y. Lee, "Collaborative deep learning model for tooth segmentation and identification using panoramic radiographs," *Computers in Biology and Medicine*, vol. 148, p. 105829, 2022.

[26] S. Hou, T. Zhou, Y. Liu, P. Dang, H. Lu, and H. Shi, "Teeth u-net: A segmentation model of dental panoramic x-ray images for

TABLE I: QUANTITATIVE COMPARISON OF DIFFERENT CNN MODULES APPLIED TO IVISIONLAB DATASET [6].

CNN Model	Evaluation Matrix					
	Jaccard index	*Recall*	*Precision*	*Accuracy*	*F1-Measure*	*F2-Measure*
U-Net++ [4]	**0.8591**	**0.9228**	0.9273	0.9715	**0.9218**	**0.9217**
ResU-Net++ [5]	0.8501	0.9098	0.9283	0.9703	0.9161	0.9115
MultiResU-Net [33]	0.8588	0.9162	**0.9339**	**0.9716**	**0.9218**	0.9176

* Bold font indicates the best value.

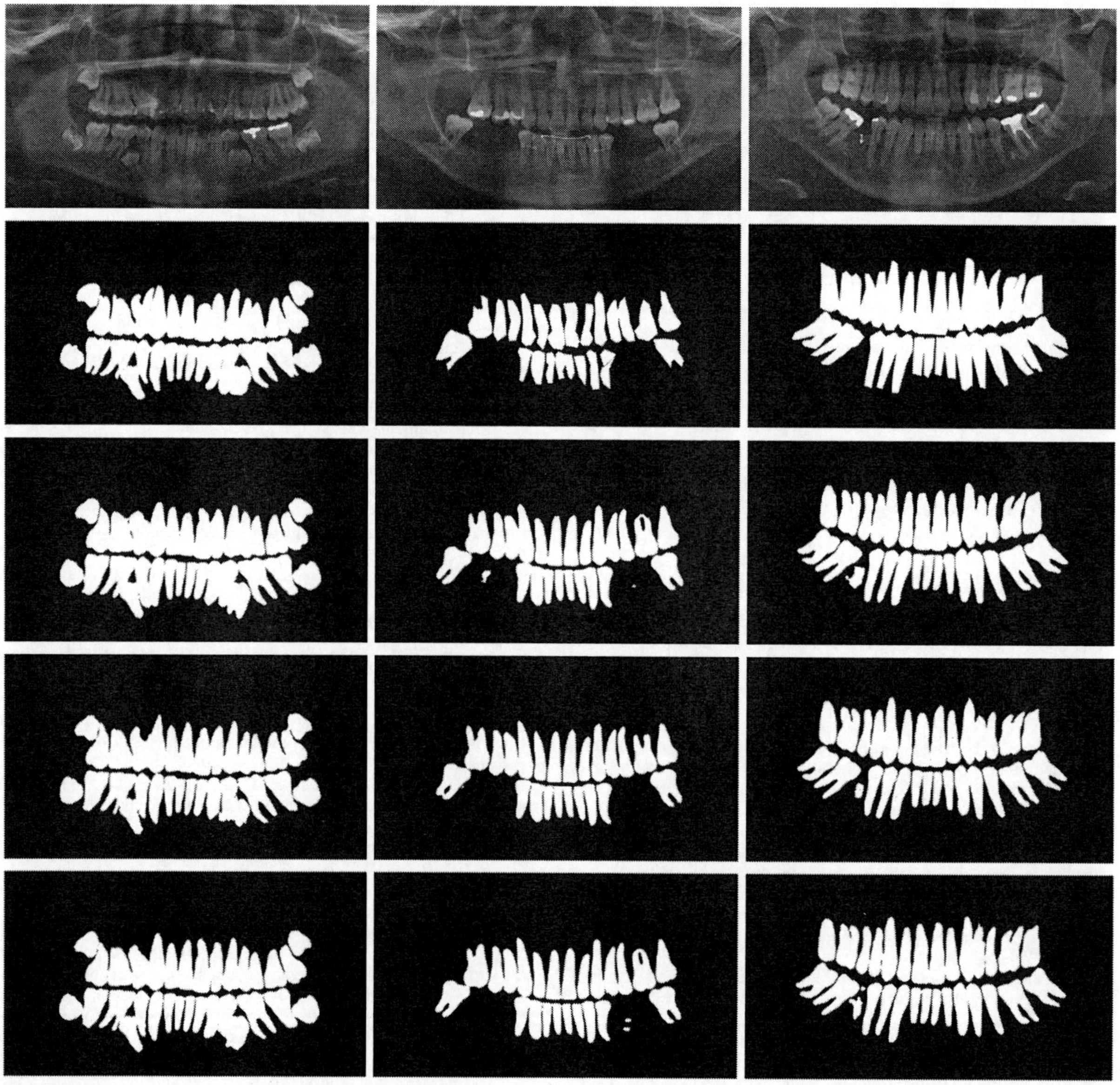

Figure 2: Qualitative analysis and comparison of the different CNN models using sample of panoramic X-ray images from IvisionLab dataset [6]. (First row): shows the original images, (Second row): ground truth, (Third row): U-Net++ [4], (Fourth row): ResU-Net++ [5] and (Fifth row): MultiResU-Net [33] segmentation results.

context semantics and contrast enhancement," *Computers in Biology and Medicine*, vol. 152, p. 106296, 2023.

[27] S. Duman, E. F. Yılmaz, G. Eşer, Ö. Çelik, I. S. Bayrakdar, E. Bilgir, A. L. F. Costa, R. Jagtap, and K. Orhan, "Detecting the presence of taurodont teeth on panoramic radiographs using a deep learning-based convolutional neural network algorithm," *Oral Radiology*, vol. 39, no. 1, pp. 207–214, 2023.

[28] A. Haghanifar, M. M. Majdabadi, S. Haghanifar, Y. Choi, and S.-B. Ko, "Paxnet: Tooth segmentation and dental caries detection in panoramic x-ray using ensemble transfer learning and capsule classifier," *Multimedia Tools and Applications*, pp. 1–21, 2023.

[29] S. M. Kahaki, M. Nordin, N. S. Ahmad, M. Arzoky, W. Ismail *et al.*, "Deep convolutional neural network designed for age assessment based on orthopantomography data," *Neural Computing and Applications*, vol. 32, no. 13, pp. 9357–9368, 2020.

[30] J. Kim, H.-S. Lee, I.-S. Song, and K.-H. Jung, "Dentnet: Deep neural transfer network for the detection of periodontal bone loss using panoramic dental radiographs," *Scientific Reports*, vol. 9, no. 1, pp. 1–9, 2019.

[31] silva. (2020) Ivisionlab, dns panoramic. [Online]. Available: https://github.com/IvisionLab/dns-panoramic-images

[32] Z. Zhang, Q. Liu, and Y. Wang, "Road extraction by deep residual u-net," *IEEE Geoscience and Remote Sensing Letters*, vol. 15, no. 5, pp. 749–753, 2018.

[33] N. Ibtehaz and M. S. Rahman, "Multiresunet: Rethinking the u-net architecture for multimodal biomedical image segmentation," *Neural Networks*, vol. 121, pp. 74–87, 2020.

[34] G. Van Rossum *et al.*, "Python programming language." in *USENIX annual technical conference*, vol. 41, no. 1, 2007, pp. 1–36.

[35] N. Ketkar and N. Ketkar, "Introduction to keras," *Deep learning with python: a hands-on introduction*, pp. 97–111, 2017.

[36] M. Abadi, P. Barham, J. Chen, Z. Chen, A. Davis, J. Dean, M. Devin, S. Ghemawat, G. Irving, M. Isard *et al.*, "Tensorflow: a system for large-scale machine learning." in *Osdi*, vol. 16, no. 2016, 2016, pp. 265–283.

Automatic Teeth Segmentation From Panoramic X-ray Images Using Deep Learning Models

Shuaa S. Alharbi
Department of Information Technology
College of Computer, Qassim University
Buraydah, Saudi Arabia
Email: shuaa.s.alharbi@qu.edu.sa

Abstract—**A dentist's primary objective when screening for X-ray problems is to determine the shape, number, and position of teeth. Computational tools have been proposed to aid specialists in making more accurate diagnoses rather than relying solely on the trained eyes of dentists. Teeth segmentation and object detection are the core functions of these tools when applied to X-ray images. Segmenting and detecting the teeth in images is actually the first step in enabling other automatic processing methods. Medical image segmentation, especially in dentistry field, has been transformed by Deep Learning (DL) in recent years. U-Net with its different extensions and modifications has been among the most popular deep networks developed for medical image segmentation. However, it is difficult to determine which one will work best for teeth segmentation. In this study, different semantic segmentation models are selected based on their common use in medical image segmentation. Models include:U-Net++, ResU-Net++ and MultiResU-Net. Using panoramic X-ray dataset, MultiResUNet architecture performed better than the other segmentation models with an accuracy of 97.16%.**

Keywords*—*Convolutional Neural Networks, Deep learning, Deep Neural Networks, Image Segmentation, Medical Image Processing, Semantic Segmentation.

I. INTRODUCTION

Artificial Intelligence (AI) is becoming increasingly popular and widely used in medical care. The application of AI in the field of dentistry has shown successful results in the dental clinic examining routine [1]. Thus, AI can be used in dentistry to detect and recognize different variables from images, such as segmenting teeth from other tissues. Even though the use of artificial intelligence has grown rapidly and widely in the health care field, its application in dental care has been relatively slow [2].

In recent years, there has been increasing interest in applying the Deep Learning (DL) models for medical image analysis. The deep learning, typically the Convolutional Neural Network (CNN, or ConvNet) has made a significant contribution to the medical images analysing tasks especially the segmentation. Semantic segmentation methods based on DL have demonstrated state-of-the-art performance over the past few years. It has been demonstrated that these techniques have been successful in classifying, segmenting, and detecting medical images. For these applications, the U-Net [3] deep learning technique has become very popular. The U-Net shape with its variations and extensions (*i.e.* U-net++ [4], Resunet++ [5]) has long been recognized as the dominant deep network architecture. In this regard, it is the most widely used architecture in the medical imaging segmentation field.

In computer-assisted procedures topically aim to applied in dental clinics, teeth segmentation is an essential step. By using this technique, it is possible to provide approximate outline images of doubtful regions in order to provide features that can distinguish tooth tissues from other types of tissues.

In this paper, we demonstrate the use of U-net shapes to improve the performance of automatic teeth segmentation from panoramic radiographs. We evaluate the performance and segmentation accuracy of these model using a pre-request dataset provided by Intelligent Vision Research Lab (Ivisionlab) alongside its ground truth [6]. Based on the results presented in this paper, these methods can be used to improve the detection and segmentation of teeth in panoramic X-ray images.

The first section discusses automatic tooth detection in panoramic images. In the second section, the methodology for evaluating the U-net algorithm is explained. Three and four sections describe the results of the evaluation experiment and the setup, respectively. In the last section, the findings of this study are summarized.

II. RELATED WORKS

In the last two decades, teeth segmentation has been the subject of research, mainly using threshold, region-based methods and and machine learning methods.

Jader *et al.*, [7] present the development of the first method for segmenting and recognizing teeth from panoramic X-ray images using a region-based CNN (R-CNN). This algorithm adds a branch for automatic recognition of object masks simultaneously with the branch for class classification and bounding box recognition [8].

In order to segment the teeth from 3D dental model, Xu *et al.*, [9] proposes an approach based upon deep convolutional neural networks for segmenting 3D dental models. Further, Tian *et al.*, [10] introduced an automated method of segmenting and describing teeth from 3D dental images by utilizing OCTREE sparse voxel technology, CRF model based on conditional random fields, and a 3D CNN named OCN [11].

Furthermore, Zhu *et al.*, [12], studied the tooth segmentation and detection of teeth using Mask R-CNN. On the basis of 100 images collected from a hospital, their method successfully distinguished between complex, crowded tooth structures. A fully (R-CNN) method for automatic tooth segmentation is being evaluated by Lee *et al.,* [13] to evaluate it using individual annotations of panoramic radiographs.

A novel feature-steered graph CNN has been developed by Sun *et al.,* in their study [14]. Using this network, individual teeth were segmented and identified from digital dental castings. Towards this goal, the framework constrains its segmentation and labeling based on the distribution of crown shapes and concave contours. This method is more accurate than other DL-based dental segmentation methods, such as PointNet [15], OCTREE-based CNN [11], and the two-phase cast segmentation methods.

In Zhao *et al.,* [16], attention networks were utilized for the segmentation of attention in a two-stage network for localizing multiple teeth from a publicly available panoramic X-ray image dataset. Silva *et al.,* [17] introduced TSAS-Net for the segmentation and localization of teeth from the panning dataset.

Using comprehensive semantic data, Cui *et al.,* [18] presented a comprehensive method for segmenting teeth based on Generative Adversarial Networks (GAN's) [19]. This paper presents a deep segmentation network based on an automatic pixel-level tooth segmentation method (ToothPix) using a conditional GAN structure (CGAN). A comparison of the ToothPix method with existing methods, such as Mask R-CNN and Pix2pix showed that it outperformed state-of-the-art methods. Furthermore, as part of their efforts to exploit 3D cone beam computed tomography (CBCT) images that are robust to metal artifacts generated by the procedure, Chung *et al.,* [20] have proposed the use of CNN for pixel-wise labeling of CBCT images.

A U-shaped deep CNN (U-Net) architecture was used by Zheng *et al.,* [2]. The authors propose a variant of the Dense U-Net that is anatomically constrained during design [3] that is designed to integrate oral anatomy knowledge with data-driven Dense U-Nets. They aim to provide an automated means of segmenting and detecting lesions in CBCT images.

In addition, the technique proposed by Yang *et al.,* in their work [21] aim to combines mathematical analysis (*i.e.*level set) with deep learning CNN in order to segment the teeth from CBCT images. Where Leite *et al.,* [22] described a methodology for combining different CNN models to assess the ability of a new AI-based tool to detect and segment teeth from panoramic radiographs. They developed a detector that detects teeth and fine-tunes the segmentation map by combining DeepLab-v3 [23] architecture and a pretrained ResNet-101 [24] to detect teeth.

A novel technique described by Chandrashekar *et al.,* [25] combines independent tooth segmentation and identification models obtained from panoramic radiographs. Through the use of tooth segmentation and identification models, their collaboration aims to improve collaborative learning. Through collaboration, segmented teeth are identified and numbered to enhance results.

A recent study by Hou *et al.,* [26] described a Teeth U-net model for the segmentation of dental panoramic X-ray images. The aim was to solve the problem of accurate segmentation of all teeth in dental panoramic images and the determination of clear boundaries between roots. As a means of recovering image features in the network, dense skip connections between the encoder and decoder are proposed through the use of multi-level connections. Where Duman *et al.,* [27] used 434 anonymized, mixed-size panoramic radiography images over the age of 13 years as data, they developed automatic tooth segmentation models using a Pytorch implementation of the U-Net model.

In terms of teeth segmentation, the transfer learning models show promising results. Haghanifar *et al.,* [28] aimed to automate the process of segmenting teeth and detecting dental caries in panoramic images by utilizing automatic diagnosis systems. Through transfer learning, the proposed model extracts relevant features from x-rays and draws predictions using a capsule network.

III. Method

The dentist uses panoramic radiographs to obtain an overview of the entire mouth and jaw, including all the teeth, in dentistry. It has been used to detect larger concerns like infections, impacted teeth, and tumors. There is a low resolution in panoramic radiography X-ray images, which contributes to noise in the images. To process dental X-ray images, it is necessary to distinguish between the ROI and backgrounds [29]. In this research we compare 3 different CNN models that used regularly in medical image segmentation task and evaluate their results using a publicly available dataset. The following repositories contain all the code used in this paper: U-net++ [30], ResUNet++ [31] and MutiResU-Net [32].

A. Dataset and Ground Truth

It is noteworthy that panoramic X-ray images provide a greater degree of patient comfort than other radiographics, such as intraoral images (bitewing and periapical), and are less invasive, while examining a greater portion of the maxilla and mandible [33]. For dental image analysis, only a few datasets of panoramic X-ray images are publicly available.

Only a few sets of dental images were available for image analysis in the past, and almost all of these were intraoral X-rays (bitewing or periapical). The UFBA-UESC dental images dataset was published by Silva *et al.,* [17] to fill this gap, and it has proven to be a valuable resource for the community. The original data set was published with annotations for semantic segmentation only, which utilizes binary masks to distinguish teeth from non-teeth pixels. Jader *et al.,* [7] modified the UFBA-UESC Dental Images dataset to include instance segmentation information, and a total of 276 images containing 32 teeth were used for training and validation, with the remaining 1224 images being used for testing. Recently, Silva *et al.,* [6] from Ivisionlab they annotated 543 images with number information (including the 276 used by Jader *et al.,* [7]) to evaluate semantic segmentation.

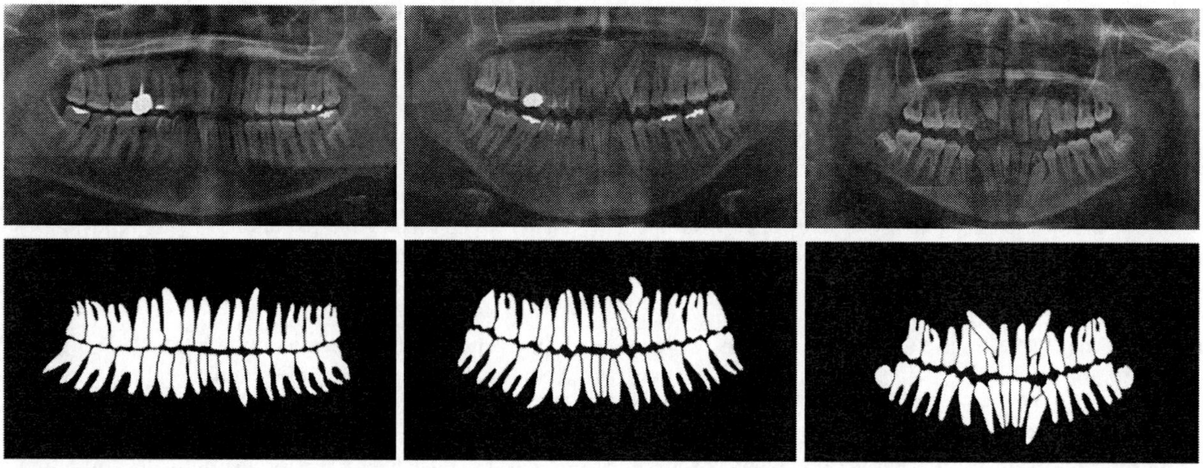

Figure 1: Three different simple panoramic X-ray images from Ivisionlab [6] alongside with their ground truth.

The dataset for this paper was obtained from Ivisionlab [6], [34] in order to perform our experiments . In this dataset, total of 1500 panoramic X-ray images with high variability have been grouped into ten categories in this dataset. It has also been updated with more instance annotations and includes information regarding numbering. A combination of panoramic X-ray images and ground truth images is included in this dataset. Figure 1 shows some samples of the dataset alongside ground truth.

B. Models Architectures Overview

1) U-net++ Architecture: The U-net++ architecture [4] in terms of medical image segmentation, is a more powerful architecture. There are several nested, dense skip pathways connecting the encoder and decoder sub-networks in this architecture. As a result of the redesign of the skip pathways, the semantic gap between the feature maps of the encoder and decoder sub-networks is reduced.

2) ResUNet++ Architecture: The ResUNet++ Architecture [5] is based on the Deep Residual U-Net (ResUNet) [35], which is a deep residual learning concept combined with an U-Net. There are three encoder blocks and three decoder blocks comprised of the ResUNet++ architecture. An encoder block comprises two successive convolutional blocks of 3×3 and an identity mapping. Using residual blocks, a deeper neural network that can solve the degradation problem in each encoder using residual blocks that propagate information over layers. Consequently, channel interdependencies are improved while computational costs are reduced.

3) MutiResU-Net Architecture: In MutiResU-Net architecture [36], a MultiRes block is proposed as a replacement for two convolutional layers. The number of filters in the convolutional layers is controlled by a parameter within each MultiRes block. A MultiRes block has been proposed in order to enhance U-Net's capability to analyze and assess data at multiple resolutions. In some cases, there is a discrepancy between the features propagated through the encoder network and the features propagated through the decoder network. In order to balance these two incompatible feature sets, MutiResU-Net offers some additional processing (*i.e.*Res paths).

IV. Results and Discussion

In this section, we present quantitative and qualitative validations using panoramic X-ray images, then compare the results with different CNNs approaches.

A. Evaluation and Assessment Metrics

In order to evaluate the predictive performance of each detection model, we use F1 and F2 scores. F1 scores are calculated by combining precision and recall, and therefore provide a more accurate measure of predictive performance than simply the percentage of correct predictions. Where F2 is defined as the weighted average mean of precision and recall (given a threshold value). A F2 score places more emphasis on recall than precision, in contrast with the F1 score, in which precision and recall are equally weighted.

A measurement of accuracy is used to determine how closely a measurement is to a standard or known value. Moreover, segmentation tasks are commonly evaluated by Dice scores and Jaccard indices in medical imaging. It is common for convolutional neural networks to be optimized for cross-entropy (weighted) when they are trained to segment images. The purpose of this measurment is essentially to quantify the overlap between our prediction output and the target mask.

The relevant mathematical expressions are as follows:

$$\text{Precision} = \frac{TP}{TP + FP} \tag{1}$$

$$\text{Recall (Sensitivity)} = \frac{TN}{TN + FP} \tag{2}$$

$$\text{F1-Measure} = \frac{2 \cdot TP}{2 \cdot TP + FP + FN} \tag{3}$$

$$\text{F2-Measure} = \frac{TP}{TP + 0.2 \cdot 0.8FN} \tag{4}$$

TABLE I: QUANTITATIVE COMPARISON OF DIFFERENT CNN MODULES APPLIED TO IVISIONLAB DATASET [6].

CNN Model	Evaluation Matrix					
	Jaccard index	*Recall*	*Precision*	*Accuracy*	*F1-Measure*	*F2-Measure*
U-Net++ [4]	**0.8591**	**0.9228**	0.9273	0.9715	**0.9218**	**0.9217**
ResU-Net++ [5]	0.8501	0.9098	0.9283	0.9703	0.9161	0.9115
MultiResU-Net [36]	0.8588	0.9162	**0.9339**	**0.9716**	**0.9218**	0.9176

* Bold font indicates the best value.

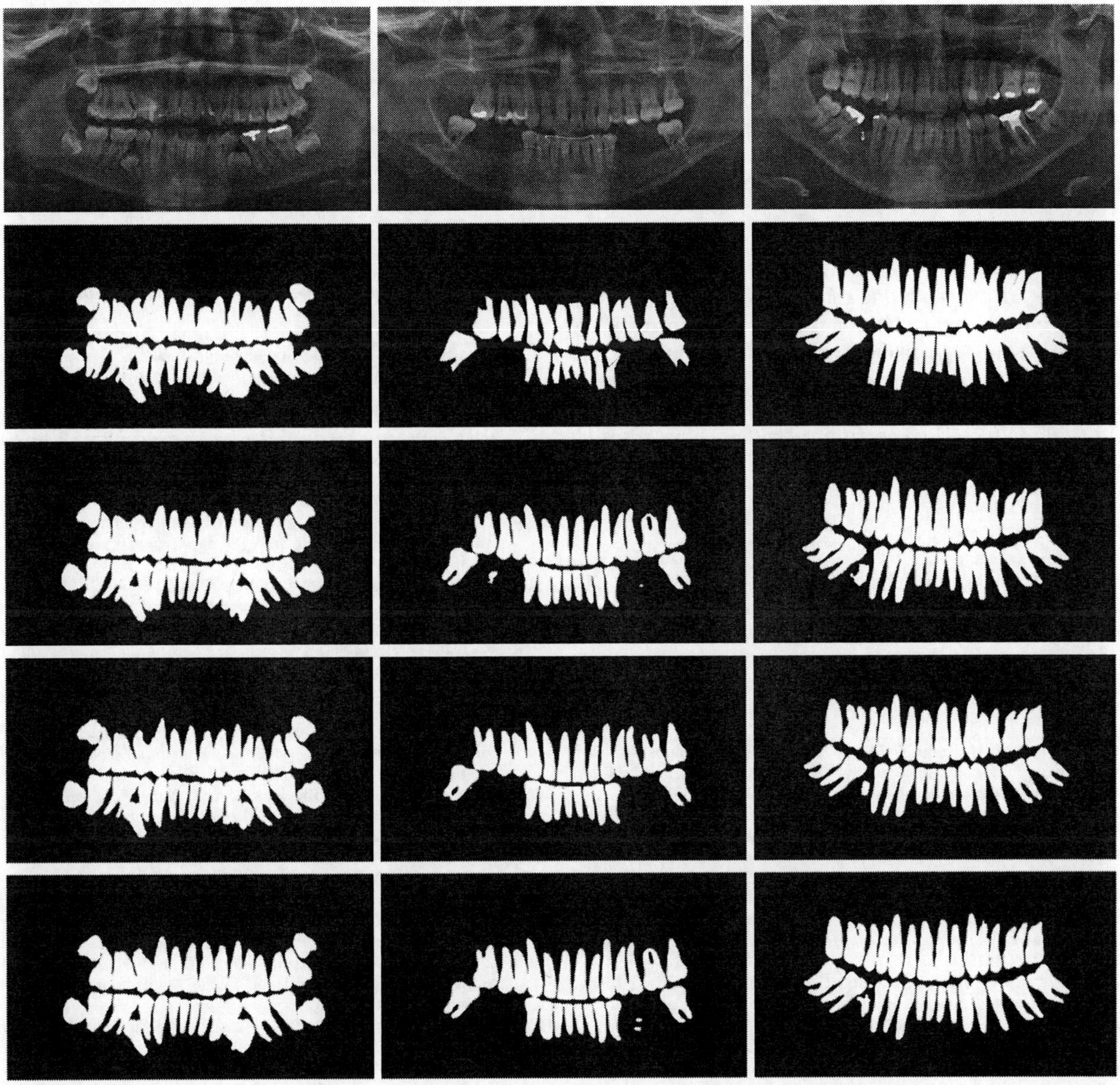

Figure 2: Qualitative analysis and comparison of the different CNN models using sample of panoramic X-ray images from IvisionLab dataset [6]. (First row): shows the original images, (Second row): ground truth, (Third row): U-Net++ [4], (Fourth row): ResU-Net++ [5] and (Fifth row): MultiResU-Net [36] segmentation results.

$$\text{Accuracy} = \frac{TP + TN}{TP + TN + FP + FN} \quad (5)$$

$$\text{Jaccard index} = \frac{TP}{TP + FN + FP} \quad (6)$$

Where TP is true positive, TN—true negative, FP—false positive, and FN—false negative cases.

B. Quantitative and Qualitative Comparison

In the following Table I and Figure 2, U-Net shape CNN models are quantitatively analyzed using IvisionLab data [6]. It is notable that MutiResU-Net outperformed compare with other methods with accuracy of 97.16%. This is because MutiResU-Net performs better on heterogeneous datasets than classical U-Net [36].

C. Experimental Setup

The experiments were conducted using Python, more specifically Python3 [37]. Where in order to construct the network models, Keras [38] was used with Tensorflow [39] as the backend.

V. Conclusion

The results of our study indicate that MutiResU-Net may succeed the other U-Net architectures in the future, particularly when it comes to segmenting teeth from panoramic X-ray images. This experiment and assumption relied on a single dataset for the evaluation of different models, which could explain why MultiResU-Net performed better. Future research should conduct experiments with different datasets to see whether this claim holds.

Acknowledgment

The author extend her appreciation to the Deputyship for Research & Innovation, Ministry of Education, and Qassim University, Saudi Arabia, for funding this research work. The author also thank Qassim University for technical support.

References

[1] D. L. Duong, M. H. Kabir, and R. F. Kuo, "Automated caries detection with smartphone color photography using machine learning," *Health Informatics Journal*, vol. 27, no. 2, p. 14604582211007530, 2021.

[2] Z. Zheng, H. Yan, F. C. Setzer, K. J. Shi, M. Mupparapu, and J. Li, "Anatomically constrained deep learning for automating dental cbct segmentation and lesion detection," *IEEE Transactions on Automation Science and Engineering*, vol. 18, no. 2, pp. 603–614, 2020.

[3] O. Ronneberger, P. Fischer, and T. Brox, "U-net: Convolutional networks for biomedical image segmentation," in *International Conference on Medical image computing and computer-assisted intervention*. Springer, 2015, pp. 234–241.

[4] Z. Zhou, M. M. Rahman Siddiquee, N. Tajbakhsh, and J. Liang, "Unet++: A nested u-net architecture for medical image segmentation," in *Deep Learning in Medical Image Analysis and Multimodal Learning for Clinical Decision Support: International Workshop, DLMIA 2018, and 8th International Workshop, ML-CDS 2018, Held in Conjunction with MICCAI 2018, Granada, Spain, September 20, 2018, Proceedings 4*, 2018, pp. 3–11.

[5] D. Jha, P. H. Smedsrud, M. A. Riegler, D. Johansen, T. De Lange, P. Halvorsen, and H. D. Johansen, "Resunet++: An advanced architecture for medical image segmentation," in *2019 IEEE International Symposium on Multimedia (ISM)*, 2019, pp. 225–2255.

[6] B. Silva, L. Pinheiro, L. Oliveira, and M. Pithon, "A study on tooth segmentation and numbering using end-to-end deep neural networks," in *Conference on Graphics, Patterns and Images (SIBGRAPI)*, 2020, pp. 164–171.

[7] G. Jader, J. Fontineli, M. Ruiz, K. Abdalla, M. Pithon, and L. Oliveira, "Deep instance segmentation of teeth in panoramic x-ray images," in *Conference on Graphics, Patterns and Images (SIBGRAPI)*, 2018, pp. 400–407.

[8] K. He, G. Gkioxari, P. Dollár, and R. Girshick, "Mask r-cnn," in *Proceedings of the IEEE international conference on computer vision*, 2017, pp. 2961–2969.

[9] X. Xu, C. Liu, and Y. Zheng, "3d tooth segmentation and labeling using deep convolutional neural networks," *IEEE transactions on visualization and computer graphics*, vol. 25, no. 7, pp. 2336–2348, 2018.

[10] S. Tian, N. Dai, B. Zhang, F. Yuan, Q. Yu, and X. Cheng, "Automatic classification and segmentation of teeth on 3d dental model using hierarchical deep learning networks," *IEEE Access*, vol. 7, pp. 84817–84828, 2019.

[11] P.-S. Wang, Y. Liu, Y.-X. Guo, C.-Y. Sun, and X. Tong, "O-cnn: Octree-based convolutional neural networks for 3d shape analysis," *ACM Transactions On Graphics (TOG)*, vol. 36, no. 4, pp. 1–11, 2017.

[12] G. Zhu, Z. Piao, and S. C. Kim, "Tooth detection and segmentation with mask r-cnn," in *2020 International Conference on Artificial Intelligence in Information and Communication (ICAIIC)*, 2020, pp. 070–072.

[13] J.-H. Lee, S.-S. Han, Y. H. Kim, C. Lee, and I. Kim, "Application of a fully deep convolutional neural network to the automation of tooth segmentation on panoramic radiographs," *Oral Surgery, Oral Medicine, Oral Pathology and Oral Radiology*, vol. 129, no. 6, pp. 635–642, 2020.

[14] D. Sun, Y. Pei, G. Song, Y. Guo, G. Ma, T. Xu, and H. Zha, "Tooth segmentation and labeling from digital dental casts," in *2020 IEEE 17th International Symposium on Biomedical Imaging (ISBI)*, 2020, pp. 669–673.

[15] C. R. Qi, H. Su, K. Mo, and L. J. Guibas, "Pointnet: Deep learning on point sets for 3d classification and segmentation," in *Proceedings of the IEEE conference on computer vision and pattern recognition*, 2017, pp. 652–660.

[16] Y. Zhao, P. Li, C. Gao, Y. Liu, Q. Chen, F. Yang, and D. Meng, "Tsasnet: Tooth segmentation on dental panoramic x-ray images by two-stage attention segmentation network," *Knowledge-Based Systems*, vol. 206, p. 106338, 2020.

[17] G. Silva, L. Oliveira, and M. Pithon, "Automatic segmenting teeth in x-ray images: Trends, a novel data set, benchmarking and future perspectives," *Expert Systems with Applications*, vol. 107, pp. 15–31, 2018.

[18] W. Cui, L. Zeng, B. Chong, and Q. Zhang, "Toothpix: Pixel-level tooth segmentation in panoramic x-ray images based on generative adversarial networks," in *International Symposium on Biomedical Imaging (ISBI)*, 2021, pp. 1346–1350.

[19] M.-Y. Liu and O. Tuzel, "Coupled generative adversarial networks," *Advances in Neural Information Processing Systems*, vol. 29, 2016.

[20] M. Chung, M. Lee, J. Hong, S. Park, J. Lee, J. Lee, I.-H. Yang, J. Lee, and Y.-G. Shin, "Pose-aware instance segmentation framework from cone beam ct images for tooth segmentation," *Computers in biology and medicine*, vol. 120, p. 103720, 2020.

[21] Y. Yang, R. Xie, W. Jia, Z. Chen, Y. Yang, L. Xie, and B. Jiang, "Accurate and automatic tooth image segmentation model with deep convolutional neural networks and level set method," *Neurocomputing*, vol. 419, pp. 108–125, 2021.

[22] A. F. Leite, A. V. Gerven, H. Willems, T. Beznik, P. Lahoud, H. Gaêta-Araujo, M. Vranckx, and R. Jacobs, "Artificial intelligence-driven novel tool for tooth detection and segmentation on panoramic radiographs," *Clinical oral investigations*, vol. 25, no. 4, pp. 2257–2267, 2021.

[23] L.-C. Chen, G. Papandreou, F. Schroff, and H. Adam, "Rethinking atrous convolution for semantic image segmentation," *arXiv preprint arXiv:1706.05587*, 2017.

[24] Y. Rao, L. He, and J. Zhu, "A residual convolutional neural network for pan-shaprening," in *2017 International Workshop on Remote Sensing with Intelligent Processing (RSIP)*. IEEE, 2017, pp. 1–4.

[25] G. Chandrashekar, S. AlQarni, E. E. Bumann, and Y. Lee, "Collaborative deep learning model for tooth segmentation and identification using panoramic radiographs," *Computers in Biology and Medicine*, vol. 148, p. 105829, 2022.

[26] S. Hou, T. Zhou, Y. Liu, P. Dang, H. Lu, and H. Shi, "Teeth u-net: A segmentation model of dental panoramic x-ray images for

context semantics and contrast enhancement," *Computers in Biology and Medicine*, vol. 152, p. 106296, 2023.
[27] S. Duman, E. F. Yılmaz, G. Eşer, Ö. Çelik, I. S. Bayrakdar, E. Bilgir, A. L. F. Costa, R. Jagtap, and K. Orhan, "Detecting the presence of taurodont teeth on panoramic radiographs using a deep learning-based convolutional neural network algorithm," *Oral Radiology*, vol. 39, no. 1, pp. 207–214, 2023.
[28] A. Haghanifar, M. M. Majdabadi, S. Haghanifar, Y. Choi, and S.-B. Ko, "Paxnet: Tooth segmentation and dental caries detection in panoramic x-ray using ensemble transfer learning and capsule classifier," *Multimedia Tools and Applications*, pp. 1–21, 2023.
[29] S. M. Kahaki, M. Nordin, N. S. Ahmad, M. Arzoky, W. Ismail *et al.*, "Deep convolutional neural network designed for age assessment based on orthopantomography data," *Neural Computing and Applications*, vol. 32, no. 13, pp. 9357–9368, 2020.
[30] MrGiovanni. (2019) U-net++. [Online]. Available: https://github.com/MrGiovanni/UNetPlusPlus
[31] DebeshJha. (2022) Resunetplusplus. [Online]. Available: https://github.com/DebeshJha/ResUNetPlusPlus
[32] Nibtehaz. (2022) Multiresunet. [Online]. Available: https://github.com/nibtehaz/MultiResUNet
[33] J. Kim, H.-S. Lee, I.-S. Song, and K.-H. Jung, "Dentnet: Deep neural transfer network for the detection of periodontal bone loss using panoramic dental radiographs," *Scientific Reports*, vol. 9, no. 1, pp. 1–9, 2019.
[34] silva. (2020) Ivisionlab, dns panoramic. [Online]. Available: https://github.com/IvisionLab/dns-panoramic-images
[35] Z. Zhang, Q. Liu, and Y. Wang, "Road extraction by deep residual u-net," *IEEE Geoscience and Remote Sensing Letters*, vol. 15, no. 5, pp. 749–753, 2018.
[36] N. Ibtehaz and M. S. Rahman, "Multiresunet: Rethinking the u-net architecture for multimodal biomedical image segmentation," *Neural Networks*, vol. 121, pp. 74–87, 2020.
[37] G. Van Rossum *et al.*, "Python programming language." in *USENIX annual technical conference*, vol. 41, no. 1, 2007, pp. 1–36.
[38] N. Ketkar and N. Ketkar, "Introduction to keras," *Deep learning with python: a hands-on introduction*, pp. 97–111, 2017.
[39] M. Abadi, P. Barham, J. Chen, Z. Chen, A. Davis, J. Dean, M. Devin, S. Ghemawat, G. Irving, M. Isard *et al.*, "Tensorflow: a system for large-scale machine learning." in *Osdi*, vol. 16, no. 2016, 2016, pp. 265–283.

Patterns for Quantum Software Development

Fabian Bühler, Johanna Barzen, Martin Beisel, Daniel Georg, Frank Leymann, and Karoline Wild
Institute of Architecture of Application Systems, University of Stuttgart
Universitätsstrasse 38, 70569 Stuttgart, Germany
email: {firstname.lastname}@iaas.uni-stuttgart.de

***Abstract*—Quantum algorithms have the potential to outperform classical algorithms for certain problems. However, implementing quantum algorithms in a reusable manner and integrating them into applications poses new challenges. To ensure reusability and integrability, quantum algorithm implementations must handle different problem sizes, be able to be processed by different quantum computers, and should also be able to be used and integrated by non-quantum experts. In classical software engineering a variety of best practices and design principles to achieve reusability of classical software components are well-known and documented as patterns. However, quantum software engineering currently lacks best practices for creating reusable implementations of quantum algorithms. To close this gap, this paper presents five patterns that describe proven solutions for modularization, integration, and translation of quantum algorithm implementations, further extending the existing quantum computing pattern language.**

***Index Terms*—Quantum Computing; Pattern Language; Quantum Software Engineering; Quantum Computing Patterns.**

I. Introduction

Quantum algorithms have the potential to outperform their classical counterparts by exploiting quantum mechanical phenomena such as entanglement. Most quantum algorithms are hybrid, comprising classical and quantum computations. This includes not only variational quantum algorithms (VQAs) [1], e.g., the Variational Quantum Eigensolver (VQE) and Quantum Approximate Optimization Algorithm (QAOA) [2], but also Shor's algorithm for prime factorization [3][4] and Grover search [5], which require classical pre- and post-processing steps and are therefore also hybrid [6].

Implementing a quantum algorithm is a complex task requiring expertise in the field of quantum computing and software engineering. Implementations consist of code that represents quantum circuits, and code defining the classical logic of the quantum algorithm. These algorithm implementations can then be integrated in hybrid quantum-classical applications [7] to solve specific problems. Thus, the reusability of implementations of quantum algorithms and their integration into applications, where their hybrid nature on the level of algorithms and applications poses additional challenges [8], are of great importance to quantum software engineering [9].

Reusability in the context of quantum algorithm implementations comprises multiple aspects: One aspect is the reusability of an implementation in different applications. The programming language used for the implementation has a large influence on its reusability, e.g., quantum algorithms implemented in a Python-based quantum programming language can easily be integrated directly into applications also implemented in Python. Another aspect is the reusability for different problem instances. Reusable implementations of quantum algorithms, e.g., to solve the maximum cut problem [10], should be able to process graphs of different sizes, which may affect the number of qubits required. Moreover, reusable algorithm implementations should be executable on different hardware, i.e., quantum computers of different vendors.

To achieve a high degree of reusability, classical software engineering provides many well-documented and well-known best practices for structuring the code of classical applications, such as modularization to achieve separation of concerns. To the best of our knowledge, similar best practices for implementing quantum algorithms and integrating them into applications are neither well-established nor well-documented in the emerging field of quantum software engineering.

An established method to document best practices for solving recurring problems are patterns [11]. They provide a structured way to capture design and architectural knowledge in a human-readable format. Patterns have been originally introduced by Alexander [12] in the domain of building architectures. Today they are widely used in different domains including software engineering, e.g., for the design of object-oriented applications [13], the integration of enterprise applications [14], or cloud computing [15]. Typically, patterns of a certain domain are organized in a pattern language. Patterns within a pattern language are interconnected, to facilitate the combination of related patterns and ease the understanding of similar problems and their solutions.

In the quantum computing domain, Leymann [16] introduced a pattern language, which has since been extended several times [2][17][18][19][20][21]. The pattern language contains patterns of different categories, e.g., patterns related to quantum operations or specific quantum algorithm classes. However, patterns documenting best practices to improve the reusability of quantum algorithm implementations are not yet part of the language. To close this gap, we extend the quantum computing pattern language by five new patterns that cover different aspects of reusability of such implementations.

The structure of this paper is as follows: Section II provides fundamentals on quantum software engineering and introduces the used pattern format and authoring process. Next, Section III explains the new patterns in detail, followed by a short discussion in Section IV. Then, related work is presented in Section V and Section VI provides a conclusion.

II. BACKGROUND

This section introduces fundamentals of quantum software engineering. Additionally, the concept of patterns, the pattern format used in this paper, and the pattern authoring process are described in more detail.

A. Quantum Software Engineering

Quantum software engineering is an emerging field that aims to apply software engineering principles to the development of applications using *quantum algorithm* implementations [22]. In particular, the reusability of such implementations is a main goal of quantum software engineering [9]. One aspect of reusability is the ability to integrate quantum algorithm implementations into different applications. Typically, quantum algorithm implementations are integrated into *hybrid quantum-classical applications* [7], or *hybrid applications* for short, to solve problems that can only be solved efficiently using a quantum computer, while classical computers are used for general purpose computation and data storage.

Most quantum algorithms are hybrid algorithms, including variational algorithms as well as all algorithms that require classical computing for pre- and post-processing [6]. Thus, a quantum algorithm implementation is divided into a *quantum part* and a *classical part*. Although both classical and quantum parts can be implemented in similar text-based programming languages, developing quantum parts requires expert knowledge of quantum computing and its mathematical foundations in addition to software engineering knowledge.

Quantum computers use unique instruction sets. To make use of synergies with the existing patterns this paper focuses on gate-based quantum computing. For the gate-based quantum computing model, *quantum gates* represent the operations performed on qubits and together with the measurements to retrieve the results of the quantum computation, they form the *quantum circuit* that can be processed by a quantum computer. However, quantum computers of different vendors support different gates natively, which can lead to vendor lock-in when implementing quantum algorithms.

The inputs of a quantum algorithm, e.g., the problem instance, must be encoded into the quantum circuit. Therefore, reusable quantum algorithm implementations require a dynamic generation of quantum circuits based on the given input.

B. Pattern Format and Authoring Method

Patterns provide proven solutions for recurring problems in a structured, human-readable manner. Alexander et al. [12] originally introduced the concept of patterns in the domain of building architectures. This concept has then been adopted by the information technology domain. For documenting patterns in this domain, Coplien [11] provides guidelines for writing software patterns. In this work, the already established pattern format of the quantum computing pattern language that follows these guidelines for documenting patterns is used.

Each pattern has a descriptive *name* and a mnemonic *icon*. A short question briefly introduces the *problem* solved by the pattern. Next, the *context* in which the problem occurs and the *forces* acting in that context are described in detail. Forces are aspects of the problem context that require special focus. Understanding these forces is crucial as solutions often cannot resolve the forces but rather balance the forces with varying tradeoffs [11]. Then, the *solution* is presented along with a solution sketch, followed by a paragraph describing the *result* of applying that solution. The solution is presented in an abstract, technology-independent manner so that it can be applied in a broad context. Finally, real world occurrences of the pattern are listed in *known uses* and relationships to patterns solving similar problems or that are recommended to be used in combination are provided in *related patterns*.

To identify patterns for quantum software engineering solving recurring problems, we empirically inspected quantum algorithm implementations of well-established libraries like Qiskit [23] and Amazon Braket [24]. Additionally, we analyzed algorithm descriptions from scientific literature and quantum computing tutorials. Moreover, we evaluated the potential applications of established best practices of classical software engineering in the context of quantum computing.

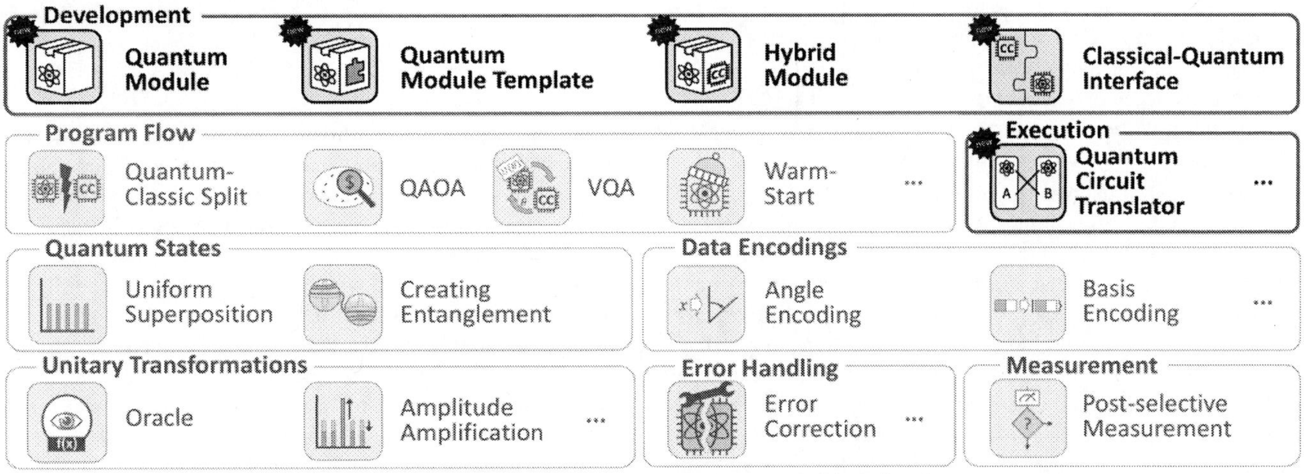

Figure 1. Overview of the quantum computing pattern language [16] including the new patterns.

III. Patterns for Quantum Software Development

As a first step to capture best practices for quantum software development and execution, five new patterns are introduced in this section that extends the existing quantum computing pattern language [2][16][17][18][19][20][21]. Figure 1 shows an overview of the categories of the quantum computing pattern language, including the new *Development* and the extended *Execution* category. The existing patterns mostly focus on the *program flow*, which uses *unitary transformations* to manipulate *quantum states*, e.g., to create specific *data encodings* for an algorithm, and *measurements* to read out the results of a quantum computation. The new patterns focus on modularization, reusability, and the integration of quantum algorithm implementations into hybrid applications.

The two patterns Quantum Module and Quantum Module Template focus on encapsulating the implementation of the quantum part of a quantum algorithm as reusable modules. Quantum Modules can generate quantum circuits with a known structure and behavior, while Quantum Module Templates allow the integration of arbitrary behavior into the generated quantum circuit. In contrast, a Hybrid Module is used to package a complete quantum algorithm implementation containing the quantum as well as the classical parts, such as the continued fraction expansion of Shor's algorithm [3], of the quantum algorithm. Its main use case is distribution and deployment of a quantum algorithm implementation for integration into hybrid applications. The implementation of a Hybrid Module can again be modularized, e.g., using Quantum Modules or Quantum Module Templates. A Classical-Quantum Interface facilitates the use of quantum algorithms by non-quantum computing experts. Last, a Quantum Circuit Translator enables the execution of quantum circuits on quantum computers of different vendors by translating the circuits into a compatible format. In the following subsections these patterns are presented in detail.

A. Quantum Module

Problem: *How can the implementation of the quantum part of a quantum algorithm be packaged for reuse independent of concrete input values?*

Context: Each quantum algorithm is a hybrid algorithm, i.e., parts of the algorithm require quantum computers and other parts require classical computers for their execution. For the execution of the quantum part, a quantum circuit implementing the required operations is needed. However, quantum circuits are problem-specific and, thus, depend on various inputs, e.g., the problem instance or initial values for parameterized quantum gates, which are then optimized by a classical optimizer. Therefore, the implementation of the quantum part of a quantum algorithm must be input-agnostic in order to be reusable.

Forces: Quantum circuits to be processed by a quantum computer must already contain all appropriately encoded input values. A static implementation of a quantum circuit that does not allow the quantum circuit to be changed based on some input values cannot be reused to solve different problems. Thus, a reusable implementation of the quantum part of a quantum algorithm needs to be able to adapt the quantum circuit to different input values. The input values that need to be encoded in a quantum circuit are, first, the problem to be solved, e.g., an implementation of Shor's algorithm [3] would require as input the number to be factored into primes, and second, parameters used for optimization or machine learning, e.g., for QAOA [2].

Moreover, implementing the quantum part of a quantum algorithm requires in depth knowledge of quantum computing and the underlying mathematical concepts. Thus, quantum computing experts are required in the development teams. However, other parts of the algorithm that only require classical computation, e.g., classical optimizers, may not require quantum computing knowledge at all and can be implemented by different teams without a quantum computing expert.

Solution: Separate the implementation of the quantum part of the quantum algorithm into one or more Quantum Modules. These modules contain the code that generates quantum circuits based on input values provided to the module. Quantum modules can also be used to reduce the number of code duplicates by implementing common parts of a quantum circuit as a reusable quantum module.

The solution sketch in Figure 2 depicts that a Quantum Module receives input values and uses generative code to construct quantum circuits depending on these input values. This ensures the reusability of the Quantum Module, as the implementation can create quantum circuits for different problem sizes as well as parameters.

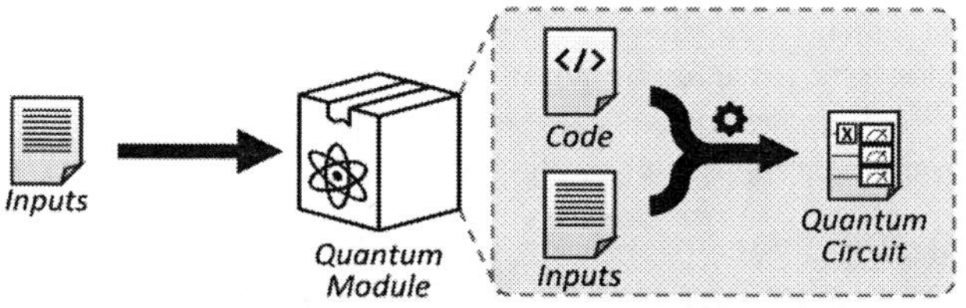

Figure 2. Solution sketch: Quantum Module.

Result: A quantum algorithm implementation is partitioned into (i) Quantum Modules containing the implementations of the quantum part, and (ii) additional classical code required for the control flow and other classical computations of the quantum algorithm. The quantum modules are independent of the concrete input values, which increases their reusability for different quantum algorithm implementations.

The separation of code that generates quantum circuits into quantum modules can thus also be reflected in the organizational structure of the development teams. Only the teams working on the quantum modules need quantum computing experts, while other teams mainly need experts in classical software engineering.

Known Uses: QUANTUM MODULES can already be found in several libraries for building quantum circuits. In Amazon Braket [24], the Grover algorithm [5] is offered as a module with functions to build the oracle and execute the Grover search. Another example of a QUANTUM MODULE for creating oracles is the *PhaseOracle* in Qiskit [23]. Generic parts used in multiple quantum algorithms, such as the quantum fourier transformation used in Shor's algorithm [3] are available in Amazon Braket [24] and Qiskit [23]. The quantum phase estimation, which is also part of Shor's algorithm can be constructed in Qiskit [23] with the *PhaseEstimation* module.
Related Patterns: A QUANTUM MODULE generating specific quantum circuits for a quantum algorithm can be used inside a HYBRID MODULE that contains the implementation of the overall quantum algorithm with its quantum and classical parts. Quantum circuits generated by a QUANTUM MODULE can be integrated into a QUANTUM MODULE TEMPLATE to create a complete quantum circuit, if the QUANTUM MODULE only generates a part of a quantum circuit. The boundary of a QUANTUM MODULE is directly corresponding to the QUANTUM-CLASSIC SPLIT [16]. The QUANTUM-CLASSIC SPLIT pattern states, that there is necessarily a separation – a split – between code executed on classical computers and code executed on quantum computers. Thus, the QUANTUM MODULE pattern is related to this pattern.

B. *Quantum Module Template*

Problem: *How can the implementation of the quantum part of a quantum algorithm be packaged for reuse when some of the behavior is determined later?*

Context: Some quantum algorithms can be implemented in a reusable manner, but their behavior may be partially modified depending on the problem to which the algorithm is applied. For example, the Grover search algorithm [5] contains an unspecified oracle. The information required for defining the concrete behavior of this oracle may not be available until a later point in time. Similar cases are algorithms like QAOA [2], which do not specify a concrete ansatz to use. Thus, implementations of the quantum part of such algorithms, where the unspecified behavior can be integrated later, are required.

Forces: Quantum algorithms may intentionally leave parts of the behavior of the quantum part unspecified until a later point in time. For example, the Grover search [5] uses an unspecified placeholder gate, as the specific function that marks the correct values cannot be known before it has been decided what to search for. In the case of QAOA, the choice of a suitable ansatz depends on information that is only available at runtime. However, for the algorithms to be executed, the missing behavior must be integrated before the execution of the quantum circuits on a quantum computer. Note, that similar situations can arise if the development of a quantum algorithm is split between different teams.

Integrating quantum behavior into an existing circuit requires a specification of the requirements an implementation has to fulfill to be integrated and function correctly. This includes the specification of the input qubits available, possible ancilla qubits, on which qubits and in what form the output is expected, and any other requirements or restrictions, e.g., on the creation of entanglement between quantum bits. Some of the restrictions, e.g., the number of available ancilla qubits, may additionally depend on the quantum computer used for execution, as a quantum computer with more qubits can allocate more ancilla qubits if the number of qubits used in the circuit is otherwise constant.
Solution: Implement the generic behavior of the quantum part of a quantum algorithm in a QUANTUM MODULE TEMPLATE. This module accepts inputs, that define the unspecified behavior to be integrated into the final quantum circuit. The behavior can either be specified as a quantum circuit or as a QUANTUM MODULE that generates the required quantum circuit. This circuit then gets integrated by the QUANTUM MODULE TEMPLATE into the main quantum circuit that represents the generic behavior.

To ensure that the *behavior* input, in form of a quantum circuit, can be integrated to correctly perform the operations it contains, the QUANTUM MODULE TEMPLATE must include specifications in the documentation that can be used to build a compatible quantum circuit, as outlined in the pattern forces. This specification is mainly a contract that needs to be fulfilled by the quantum circuit serving as input for the template. Similar contracts, e.g., plugin contracts [25], are also used in classical software engineering.

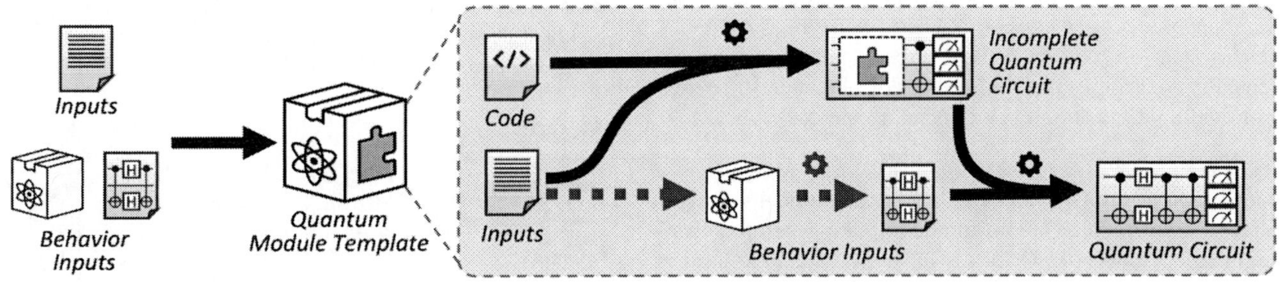

Figure 3. Solution sketch: QUANTUM MODULE TEMPLATE.

Figure 3 sketches the essential building blocks of a Quantum Module Template. The template requires two kinds of inputs: (i) the input values representing the problem to be solved as well as parameters affecting the circuit generation, as used in the Quantum Module, and (ii) behavior inputs partially specifying the behavior of the algorithm, provided in the form of a quantum circuit or a Quantum Module. Much like the Quantum Module, the Quantum Module Template uses the input values to generate a quantum circuit, which is still incomplete as it does not include the behavior from the behavior inputs yet. If the behavior inputs are provided in the form of a quantum module, this module is used to generate a quantum circuit from the inputs. Finally, the quantum circuit is integrated into the incomplete main circuit. However, implementations of the template are not limited to the exemplary steps shown here.

Result: The generic behavior of the quantum part of a quantum algorithm is implemented as Quantum Module Template that requires behavior inputs to generate an executable complete quantum circuit. The behavior inputs specify the parts of the algorithm's behavior that cannot be known in advance. Thereby, their influence on the resulting quantum circuit can be significantly higher than with a Quantum Module. The behavior inputs must be compatible with the required input definitions of the template.

The integration of the behavior inputs can be done at design time if the behavior is provided as Quantum Module, since the Quantum Module generates the circuit based on the input values. Templates can be nested inside other templates to compose quantum circuits from Quantum Modules implementing higher level circuit functions. This facilitates the replacement of a part of a quantum circuit if that part should be generated by a new Quantum Module implementing an improved algorithm, e.g., a more efficient state preparation.

Known Uses: Various quantum algorithms, e.g., the algorithm of Deutsch [26] or the Grover search [5], use an unspecified unitary gate as placeholder. Implementations of the generic behavior of these algorithms are available in Amazon Braket [24] and Qiskit [23]. These algorithms need oracle circuits to replace the placeholder gate, which are described in the Oracle pattern [16]. The oracle replacement is described in [27] in an *Oracle Expansion Task* for workflows using the *Quantum Modeling Extension*. Generic parts of QAOA [2], such as state preparation and the mixer operator are implemented in Amazon Braket [24] and Qiskit [23] and can be used by providing a quantum circuit encoding the cost function.

Related Patterns: A Quantum Module Template is a special kind of Quantum Module that additionally accepts behavior inputs, which are integrated into the generated quantum circuit. Quantum Module Templates can be used to integrate, e.g., Oracles [16] and State Preparation [16] circuits into an executable quantum circuit allowing circuits to be built from smaller modules.

C. Hybrid Module

Problem: *How can the implementation of a quantum algorithm requiring both classical and quantum computations be packaged so that it can be integrated into applications?*

Context: Quantum algorithms often require classical computation for pre- and post-processing of the quantum computation results [6]. This means that almost all quantum algorithms are hybrid. Thus, any implementation of a quantum algorithm has to contain both the quantum and the classical parts for the algorithm to be functional.

Forces: Quantum algorithms typically require a classical computer for some parts of their computation. This means that they can have multiple quantum and classical parts. For example, VQAs, such as VQE and QAOA, alternate between quantum and classical computations [1][2]. Both, the quantum and the classical part, are required for the algorithm to work correctly. This also includes the control flow of the algorithm, which is included in the classical part of the algorithm.

Integrating a quantum algorithm into an application requires the implementation of the entire algorithm. A dedicated interface is required to enable the integration into applications. Deploying the algorithm to a hybrid runtime, which can execute both the quantum and the classical part of the algorithm, even requires both parts to be deployed together.

Solution: Package the entire quantum algorithm, i.e., both the quantum parts and the classical parts, as a Hybrid Module. This module can be composed of smaller modules, e.g., Quantum Modules. It also contains the control flow logic to orchestrate the quantum and classical computation. The Hybrid Module should provide an interface that facilitates its integration into applications. This interface should mainly accept the required problem-specific input values, i.e., the problem that should be processed by the algorithm. Moreover, the interface of a Hybrid Module can also allow behavior inputs to the classical as well as quantum computation, similar to the Quantum Module Templates.

An exemplary sketch of a Hybrid Module is shown in Figure 4. It includes the control flow logic and implementations of classical and quantum parts with a loop between quantum and classical computation. The implementation of such a hybrid module can consist of multiple smaller modules, e.g., the three classical and one quantum computation steps shown can each be implemented in a separate module.

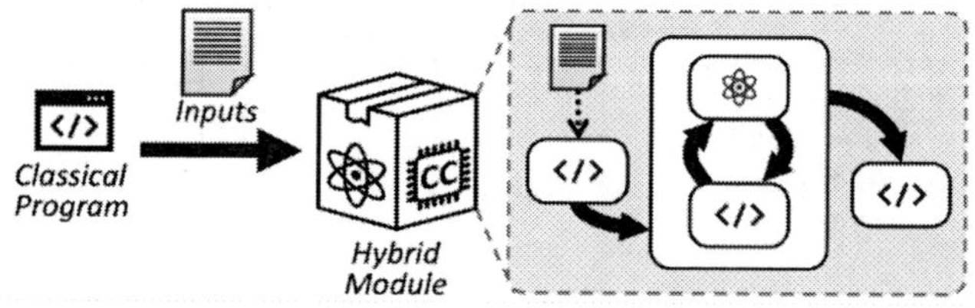

Figure 4. Solution sketch: Hybrid Module.

Result: The entire quantum algorithm implementation is packaged as a Hybrid Module. It contains both the quantum and the classical parts, as well as the control flow logic. Hybrid Modules can be used to deploy the algorithm as a standalone service, e.g., in a hybrid runtime environment that can execute both the classical and the quantum part [28]. Furthermore, a Hybrid Module can be distributed as a library that implements the quantum algorithm and can be integrated into classical applications. It provides an interface for the application to use. To facilitate the integration of a Hybrid Module by problem-domain experts, a Classical-Quantum Interface can be used as the modules' interface.
Known Uses: One concrete example are implementations of Shor's algorithm [3] which computes the prime factors of the input number. The period-finding calculated on the quantum computer and the classical post-processing performing the continued fraction expansion is packaged as a Hybrid Module in Amazon Braket [24], Qiskit [23] and Q# [29].

Other examples of Hybrid Modules are implementations of VQAs [1], e.g., QAOA and VQE implementations for the Qiskit Runtime contain the full quantum algorithm implementation [23]. Beisel et al. [30] showcase a service ecosystem enabling a workflow-based composition of Hybrid Modules for VQAs.
Related Patterns: The quantum part of the algorithm implementation inside a Hybrid Module can be organized into Quantum Modules and Quantum Module Templates. To facilitate their integration into applications by problem-domain experts without quantum computing knowledge, the Hybrid Module can expose a problem domain-specific Classical-Quantum Interface.

D. Classical-Quantum Interface

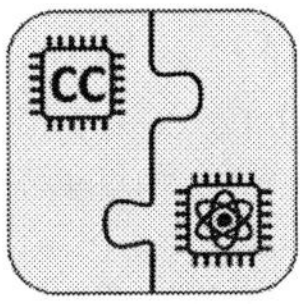

Problem: *How can a quantum algorithm implementation be used by developers without quantum computing knowledge?*

Context: Using a quantum algorithm implementation often requires in depth quantum computing knowledge. For example, the Grover search algorithm requires that the user provides a quantum circuit for the missing oracle [5]. Other algorithms, like QAOA, require choosing an ansatz, which also requires quantum computing knowledge [1][2]. However, software developers who want to integrate a quantum algorithm implementation into an application have a deep understanding of the problem domain rather than deep knowledge of quantum computing.
Forces: To integrate a quantum algorithm implementation into an application, a compatible interface is required. A Hybrid Module already provides an interface enabling its integration into applications, however, using this interface may still require considerable quantum computing knowledge. For example, it may require the problem instance to be provided in the form of a behavior input to the quantum part of an algorithm, or it may have parameters that otherwise influence the quantum part, e.g., by enabling certain error mitigation methods. The effects of the changes, e.g., on resource requirements or runtime, are difficult to estimate without knowledge of quantum computers. Thus, to facilitate the integration of quantum algorithms by problem-domain experts without quantum computing knowledge, such an interface is not sufficient.
Solution: Use a Classical-Quantum Interface that hides the quantum implementation details. Inputs can be provided to the interface in formats specific to the problem domain. These problem domain-specific inputs are internally converted into inputs in the formats required by the implementation of the quantum part.

The documentation of interface inputs that affect the quantum part requires special consideration, since understanding their impact on algorithm execution is important information when integrating the quantum algorithm implementation. Thus, the impact of these inputs on the algorithm should be documented in a comprehensible and easily understandable manner by the interface developer. For example, a parameter that increases the accuracy of the result, but also increases the number of gates in the generated circuits, which can result in increased errors with current quantum computers, could be documented as follows: *"Increasing this parameter can increase the accuracy of the result. However, it also increases the probability of computation errors accumulating, which can negate any improvement in accuracy."*

Figure 5 shows the interaction of a classical program with a quantum algorithm implemented as a Hybrid Module through a Classical-Quantum Interface. It transforms the problem domain-specific input of the classical program into the inputs required by the quantum algorithm. This interface can also be integrated directly into the Hybrid Module.

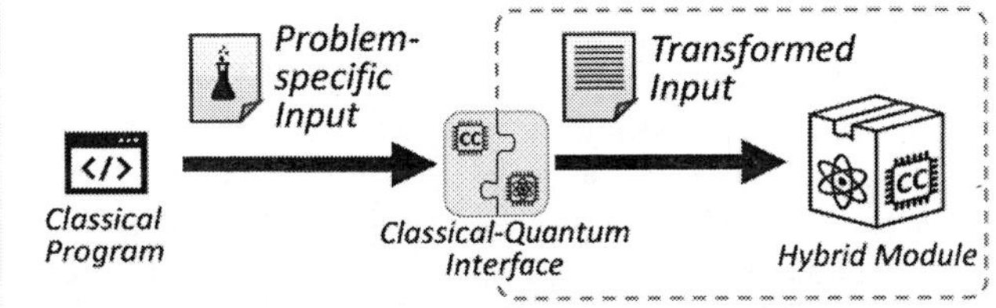

Figure 5. Solution sketch: Classical-Quantum Interface.

Result: The quantum algorithm implementation can be utilized using a Classical-Quantum Interface. Problem domain experts can make use of this quantum algorithm implementation through the Classical-Quantum Interface created for their domain. The knowledge required to utilize the algorithm implementation is presented in the interface documentation, and the format of input parameters is familiar to problem-domain experts.
Known Uses: Domain-specific libraries for quantum computing are among the first having implemented this pattern. Examples for already implemented Classical-Quantum Interfaces can be found in the chemistry domain in Qiskit, Amazon Braket, and Q# [31][32][33]. They offer transformation modules that map the electronic structure of molecules to qubits. Furthermore, Qiskit [23] provides a finance module

enabling portfolio optimization by implementing a transformer that takes a generic optimization problem as input and outputs a cost operator that can be used in a quantum algorithm. As many classical problems can be formulated as such an optimization problem, this can be used as a CLASSICAL-QUANTUM INTERFACE for different problem domains.
Related Patterns: The CLASSICAL-QUANTUM INTERFACE enables the integration of quantum algorithm implementations into applications. It can be used as an interface for a quantum algorithm implemented as a HYBRID MODULE. This interface provides a bridge between the different programming paradigms separated by the QUANTUM-CLASSIC SPLIT [16]. It is a special kind of FACADE [13] for quantum algorithms that not only hides the complexity of the algorithm, but also translates between the quantum computing domain and the problem domain.

E. Quantum Circuit Translator

Problem: *How can a quantum circuit be executed by different quantum computers with different instruction sets?*

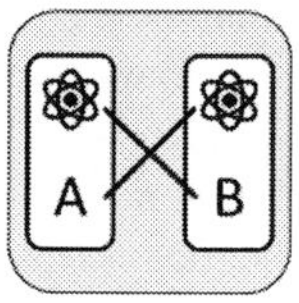

Context: Quantum circuits can be implemented in different programming languages and with different quantum gates. However, quantum computers typically only support specific circuit formats and instruction sets, which hinders interoperability and leads to vendor lock-in [34]. Thus, executing a quantum circuit on different quantum computers often requires a translation of the quantum circuit.
Forces: There are a multitude of quantum programming languages available for implementing quantum algorithms [7]. A quantum circuit may be implemented in a programming language that is incompatible with the targeted quantum computer. The circuit needs to be re-implemented in a compatible quantum programming language and instruction set. However, a manual re-implementation is error-prone, time-consuming, and requires expertise in quantum computing, and, hence, is not feasible for real-world problem sizes. Therefore, an automatic translation, transforming unsupported gates into gates natively supported by the quantum computer, is required.
Solution: Use a translator to convert the quantum circuit into the target language and transpile the circuit to the target instruction set, i.e., replace unsupported gates with equivalent gates from the target instruction set.

The solution sketch in Figure 6 shows the application of a QUANTUM CIRCUIT TRANSLATOR that translates a quantum circuit between two programming languages and instruction sets. The SWAP gate connecting the outer qubit wires in the left quantum circuit has been decomposed into three C-NOT gates in the right target quantum circuit.
Result: A QUANTUM CIRCUIT TRANSLATOR is able to automatically translate a quantum circuit into a target format, enabling components with different circuit formats and instruction sets to use the same circuit. A QUANTUM CIRCUIT TRANSLATOR increases the reusability of QUANTUM MODULES, as it enables their use with different quantum computers. However, the translated circuits do not need to be executed directly, but can instead be used as inputs for a QUANTUM MODULE TEMPLATE. Therefore, a QUANTUM CIRCUIT TRANSLATOR enables the composition of quantum algorithms based on modules implemented in different programming languages. Thus, a QUANTUM CIRCUIT TRANSLATOR can be used to increase the interoperability of QUANTUM MODULES.

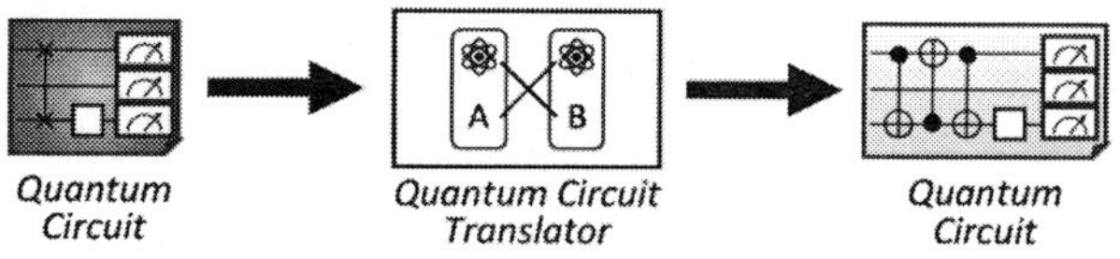

Figure 6. Solution sketch: QUANTUM CIRCUIT TRANSLATOR.

Known Uses: A widely used format for defining quantum circuits is OpenQASM [35], an open quantum assembly language. It can be imported and exported by many quantum software development kits (SDKs) such as Amazon Braket [24], Qiskit [23] and Cirq [36]. For estimating whether a quantum circuit can be executed, the *NISQ Analyzer* [34] needs the transpiled circuit for the respective quantum device. It includes multiple circuit translators. For the Python SDK Pennylane [37] there is a plugin enabling the support for IBM quantum computers without additional libraries. Explicit translation is supported by pytket [38] from and to Cirq [36]. Qconvert [39] can convert from pyQuil or OpenQASM to several other formats by using their web tool.
Related Patterns: The QUANTUM CIRCUIT TRANSLATOR pattern is related to the MESSAGE TRANSLATOR pattern from the enterprise integration pattern language [14]. With a CANONICAL DATA MODEL [14] quantum circuits of any language can be translated into any other language using at most two translators for each language. A circuit translator can be used to translate circuits generated by a QUANTUM MODULE implemented in one programming language before using them with a QUANTUM MODULE TEMPLATE implemented in a different programming language.

IV. DISCUSSION

The validity of a software engineering pattern strongly depends on the number of real-world uses of that pattern [11]. Each of the newly introduced patterns has a number of known real-world uses documented in the known uses section.

Except for quantum computing libraries aiming for a larger user base such as Qiskit, most quantum software development is currently ad-hoc, e.g., for a one-time experimental algorithm implementation without applying best practices from classical software engineering. The prevalence of ad-hoc development can be partly explained by the fact that only today's largest quantum computers have surpassed the amount of qubits that can be simulated on a classical computer [28]. Additionally, these qubits are still noisy, which further limits their potential applications [6]. Therefore, most quantum algorithms cannot show their quantum advantage for relevant problem sizes on today's quantum computers. Thus, current implementations of quantum algorithms are often single-use, e.g., for a proof-of-concept, as the limited hardware available today can only process small problems. Therefore, the majority of examples of the QUANTUM MODULE and HYBRID MODULE patterns have been found in the larger quantum computing libraries. As stated above, implementing quantum algorithms requires a deep understanding of quantum computing, its mathematical foundations, and software engineering, which is a rare combination of skills. Thus, many implementations are created by physicists without a software engineering background.

Quantum algorithms are expected to be an essential part of many applications in various domains once they can solve problems of relevant size. Since applications integrating quantum algorithms do not depend on the algorithms' implementation details, the HYBRID MODULE pattern that can hide all this complexity inside the module will be useful here.

Splitting the implementation of an algorithm into multiple modules is an established technique used to reduce the complexity of an implementation. To refine this established design principle with quantum computing-specific requirements, we introduced the module patterns to the growing quantum software engineering discipline. The two patterns, QUANTUM MODULE and QUANTUM MODULE TEMPLATE, can be used to modularize quantum algorithm implementations. Modularization can be used on multiple levels. For example, QUANTUM MODULES can be used to build a HYBRID MODULE.

To ensure the interoperability of modules, they must expose an interface that can be used by other modules. A well-defined interface improves reusability and hides complexity, such that quantum algorithm implementations can be used without deep quantum computing knowledge. The CLASSICAL-QUANTUM INTERFACE pattern is crucial for creating algorithm implementations that ease the integration into existing applications.

The last pattern, the QUANTUM CIRCUIT TRANSLATOR, is mainly used for executing quantum circuits on different quantum computers. It is required as hardware vendors have not agreed upon a standard format for representing quantum circuits. OpenQASM [35] is at the moment the most promising candidate for such a format. However, even if all existing quantum computers can interpret OpenQASM, we will most likely still have many quantum programming languages with different properties. A QUANTUM CIRCUIT TRANSLATOR that translates quantum circuits between two such languages can also be used during the development of quantum algorithms. With such a translator it becomes possible to use QUANTUM MODULES implemented in other programming languages.

V. RELATED WORK

The patterns introduced in this work extend the existing quantum computing pattern language originally introduced by Leymann [16] which is continuously growing [2][17][18][19][20][21]. There are also other publications defining terms and summarizing concepts in the quantum computing domain [40][41]. However, these concepts are not documented as patterns in the sense of the definition provided by Alexander et al. [12] to guide developers in implementing quantum algorithms. Furthermore, Huang et al. [42] describe methods for validating quantum programs using anti-patterns.

Similar approaches documented for the field of quantum computing are also established in other areas of information technology. The QUANTUM CIRCUIT TRANSLATOR is based on the same concept as the MESSAGE TRANSLATOR presented in the enterprise integration patterns by Hohpe and Woolf [14]. It enables the communication between systems using different message formats. Other related enterprise integration patterns, such as the CANONICAL DATA MODEL and the NORMALIZER, can also be adapted to the quantum computing domain.

Leymann and Barzen [43] present the Pattern Atlas, a publicly available [44] tool to facilitate the visualization of connections between patterns within a pattern language as well as between different pattern languages. Moreover, it enables the creation of *Pattern Views* [45], i.e., a collection combining individual patterns and connections from different languages.

Sánches et al. [46] define the term *quantum module* and its properties to describe how to modularize the design of quantum circuits. The QUANTUM MODULE pattern defined in our work differs significantly, as it includes classical code to generate quantum circuits. However, the properties they identified for their quantum module definition must also be fulfilled by any behavior inputs to QUANTUM MODULE TEMPLATES.

Piattini et al. [9] outline the importance of quantum software engineering. They provide principles of quantum software engineering, e.g., that quantum software has a hybrid nature and suggest that reusable parts of quantum applications should be identified for creating libraries and to provide reference examples. The patterns presented in this work can be a part of the answer towards creating reusable quantum algorithm implementations. Beisel et al. [30] modularize recurring tasks of VQAs in various microservices and integrate them using workflows. Thereby, they follow established engineering concepts to provide VQAs as reusable, automatically executable workflows. Hence, their approach is an exemplary implementation of a HYBRID MODULE.

Georg et al. [21] describe the execution of quantum applications. The PRE-DEPLOYED EXECUTION and the PRIORITIZED EXECUTION pattern can be applied to execute a quantum application created by using the HYBRID MODULE pattern, which packages the algorithm together with classical dependencies inside a single module.

The quantum software lifecycle proposed by Weder et al. [22] describes the development process of quantum applications in ten phases. The patterns in this work document best practices for the implementation phases with more detailed instructions, e.g., for the *Hardware-independent Implementation* phase by providing a QUANTUM MODULE which has a generative classical part for building the quantum circuit, or for the *Quantum Circuit Enrichment* phase by using the QUANTUM MODULE and QUANTUM MODULE TEMPLATE to better split the responsibility for the implementation of oracles and state preparation.

VI. Conclusion and Future Work

Due to the novelty of quantum computing, there are so far few, if any, established principles for quantum software development. Implementing a quantum algorithm requires expert knowledge in quantum computing and software engineering, which makes it a multidisciplinary task. Currently, quantum applications are often implemented ad hoc by physicists without in-depth software engineering knowledge. Thus, this work extends the quantum computing pattern language by five new patterns to support quantum software engineers in their work by making relevant knowledge easily accessible and digestible. The four patterns in the development category, aiding developers in creating modularized and reusable implementations of quantum algorithms, incorporate knowledge from classical software engineering adapted to the quantum computing domain. The fifth pattern, Quantum Circuit Translator, is part of the execution category and enables quantum circuits to be executed on quantum computers of different vendors. Its main use case is related to the execution of quantum circuits, but it can also be used during development.

In the future, we will make the patterns available through the Pattern Atlas [43] repository integrated into the PlanQK platform [47]. This repository already contains all previously published patterns. By introducing the patterns to the public, we can receive valuable feedback in order to further refine the existing patterns. It allows a continuous re-evaluation of the patterns, including an analysis of the usability of the patterns. Especially in such a new and rapidly growing domain as quantum software engineering, any pattern language can be expected to evolve with the domain as new best practices emerge over time. Additionally, we plan to build a quantum computing solution language [48] that can provide concrete solutions to the problems presented in the pattern language.

Acknowledgements

This work was partially funded by the BMWK projects *SeQuenC* (01MQ22009B), *EniQmA* (01MQ22007B), and *PlanQK* (01MK20005N).

References

[1] M. Cerezo *et al.*, "Variational quantum algorithms," *Nature Reviews Physics*, vol. 3, no. 9, pp. 625–644, Aug. 2021.

[2] M. Weigold, J. Barzen, F. Leymann, and D. Vietz, "Patterns for Hybrid Quantum Algorithms," in *Proceedings of the 15th Symposium and Summer School on Service-Oriented Computing (SummerSOC 2021)*. Springer International Publishing, Sep. 2021, pp. 34–51.

[3] P. W. Shor, "Polynomial-Time Algorithms for Prime Factorization and Discrete Logarithms on a Quantum Computer," *SIAM Journal on Computing*, vol. 26, no. 5, pp. 1484–1509, oct 1997.

[4] J. Barzen and F. Leymann, "Continued Fractions and Probability Estimations in Shor's Algorithm: A Detailed and Self-Contained Treatise," *AppliedMath*, vol. 2, no. 3, pp. 393–432, Jul. 2022.

[5] L. K. Grover, "A fast quantum mechanical algorithm for database search," in *Proceedings of the twenty-eighth annual ACM symposium on Theory of computing*, 1996, pp. 212–219.

[6] F. Leymann and J. Barzen, "The bitter truth about gate-based quantum algorithms in the NISQ era," *Quantum Science and Technology*, pp. 1–28, Sep. 2020.

[7] D. Vietz, J. Barzen, F. Leymann, and K. Wild, "On Decision Support for Quantum Application Developers: Categorization, Comparison, and Analysis of Existing Technologies," in *Computational Science – ICCS 2021*. Springer International Publishing, Jun. 2021, pp. 127–141.

[8] B. Weder, J. Barzen, F. Leymann, and M. Zimmermann, "Hybrid Quantum Applications Need Two Orchestrations in Superposition: A Software Architecture Perspective," in *Proceedings of the 18th IEEE International Conference on Web Services (ICWS 2021)*. IEEE, Sep. 2021, pp. 1–13.

[9] M. Piattini *et al.*, "The Talavera Manifesto for Quantum Software Engineering and Programming," Mar. 2020.

[10] E. Farhi, J. Goldstone, and S. Gutmann, "A Quantum Approximate Optimization Algorithm," Nov. 2014, arXiv:1411.4028.

[11] J. O. Coplien, *Software Patterns*. SIGS Books & Multimedia, 1996.

[12] C. Alexander, S. Ishikawa, and M. Silverstein, *A Pattern Language: Towns, Buildings, Construction*. Oxford University Press, Aug. 1977.

[13] E. Gamma, R. Helm, R. Johnson, and J. Vlissides, *Design Patterns: Elements of Reusable Object-oriented Software*. Addison-Wesley, Oct. 1994.

[14] G. Hohpe and B. Woolf, *Enterprise Integration Patterns: Designing, Building, and Deploying Messaging Solutions*. Addison-Wesley, 2004.

[15] C. Fehling, F. Leymann, R. Retter, W. Schupeck, and P. Arbitter, *Cloud Computing Patterns: Fundamentals to Design, Build, and Manage Cloud Applications*. Springer International Publishing, Jan. 2014.

[16] F. Leymann, "Towards a Pattern Language for Quantum Algorithms," in *First International Workshop, QTOP 2019, Munich, Germany, March 18, 2019, Proceedings*. Springer International Publishing, Apr. 2019, pp. 218–230.

[17] M. Weigold, J. Barzen, F. Leymann, and M. Salm, "Data Encoding Patterns For Quantum Algorithms," in *Proceedings of the 27th Conference on Pattern Languages of Programs (PLoP '20)*. HILLSIDE, Oct. 2020, pp. 1–11.

[18] M. Weigold, J. Barzen, F. Leymann, and M. Salm, "Encoding patterns for quantum algorithms," *IET QuantumCommunication*, vol. 2, no. 4, pp. 141–152, Dec. 2021.

[19] M. Weigold, J. Barzen, F. Leymann, and M. Salm, "Expanding data encoding patterns for quantum algorithms," in *2021 IEEE 18th International Conference on Software Architecture Companion (ICSA-C)*. IEEE, Mar. 2021, pp. 95–101.

[20] M. Beisel *et al.*, "Patterns for Quantum Error Handling," in *Proceedings of the 14th International Conference on Pervasive Patterns and Applications (PATTERNS 2022)*. Xpert Publishing Services (XPS), Apr. 2022, pp. 22–30.

[21] D. Georg *et al.*, "Execution Patterns for Quantum Applications," in *Proceedings of the 18th International Conference on Software Technologies (ICSOFT 2023)*. SciTePress, 2023, accepted.

[22] B. Weder, J. Barzen, F. Leymann, M. Salm, and D. Vietz, "The Quantum Software Lifecycle," in *Proceedings of the 1st ACM SIGSOFT International Workshop on Architectures and Paradigms for Engineering Quantum Software (APEQS 2020)*. ACM, Nov. 2020, pp. 2–9.

[23] Qiskit, "Qiskit: An Open-source Framework for Quantum Computing," https://qiskit.org/documentation/, [accessed: 2023.05.25].

[24] AWS, "Amazon Braket Usage Overview," https://docs.aws.amazon.com/braket/latest/developerguide/braket-using.html, [accessed: 2023.05.25].

[25] K. Marquardt, "Patterns for Plug-ins," in *Proceedings of the Fourth European Conference on Pattern Languages of Programming and Computing*, 1999.

[26] D. Collins, K. W. Kim, and W. C. Holton, "Deutsch-Jozsa algorithm as a test of quantum computation," *Phys. Rev. A*, vol. 58, pp. R1633–R1636, Sep 1998.

[27] B. Weder, U. Breitenbücher, F. Leymann, and K. Wild, "Integrating Quantum Computing into Workflow Modeling and Execution," in *Proceedings of the 13th IEEE/ACM International Conference on Utility and Cloud Computing (UCC 2020)*. IEEE, Dec. 2020, pp. 279–291.

[28] H. Riel, "Quantum Computing Technology and Roadmap," in *ESSDERC 2022 - IEEE 52nd European Solid-State Device Research Conference (ESSDERC)*, 2022, pp. 25–30.

[29] Microsoft, "Microsoft Quantum Development Kit Overview," https://learn.microsoft.com/en-us/azure/quantum/overview-what-is-qsharp-and-qdk, [accessed: 2023.05.25].

[30] M. Beisel *et al.*, "Quokka: A Service Ecosystem for Workflow-Based Execution of Variational Quantum Algorithms," in *Service-Oriented Computing – ICSOC 2022 Workshops*. Springer, Mar. 2023,

Demonstration, pp. 369–373. [Online]. Available: https://link.springer.com/chapter/10.1007/978-3-031-26507-5_35
[31] Qiskit, "Qiskit Nature Overview," https://qiskit.org/documentation/nature/index.html, [accessed: 2023.05.25].
[32] AWS, "Amazon Braket Chemistry Example," https://github.com/aws/amazon-braket-examples/blob/main/examples/hybrid_quantum_algorithms/VQE_Chemistry/VQE_chemistry_braket.ipynb, [accessed: 2023.05.25].
[33] Microsoft, "Microsoft Quantum Development Kit: Quantum Chemistry Library," https://learn.microsoft.com/en-us/azure/quantum/user-guide/libraries/chemistry/, [accessed: 2023.05.25].
[34] M. Salm *et al.*, "The NISQ Analyzer: Automating the Selection of Quantum Computers for Quantum Algorithms," in *Proceedings of the 14th Symposium and Summer School on Service-Oriented Computing (SummerSOC 2020)*. Springer International Publishing, Dec. 2020, pp. 66–85.
[35] A. Cross *et al.*, "OpenQASM 3: A Broader and Deeper Quantum Assembly Language," *ACM Transactions on Quantum Computing*, vol. 3, no. 3, pp. 1–50, Sep. 2022.
[36] Google, "Cirq," https://quantumai.google/cirq, [accessed: 2023.05.25].
[37] V. Bergholm *et al.*, "PennyLane: Automatic differentiation of hybrid quantum-classical computations," 2018, arxiv:1811.04968.
[38] Cambridge Quantum, Quantum Software and Technologies, "Pytket Extensions," https://github.com/CQCL/pytket-cirq, [accessed: 2023.05.25].
[39] Quantastica, "Quantum programming language converter," https://github.com/quantastica/qconvert, [accessed: 2023.05.25].
[40] S. Perdrix, "Quantum patterns and types for entanglement and separability," *Electronic Notes in Theoretical Computer Science*, vol. 170, pp. 125–138, 2007.
[41] S. S. Gill *et al.*, "Quantum Computing: A Taxonomy, Systematic Review and Future Directions," 2020, arxiv:2010.15559.
[42] Y. Huang and M. Martonosi, "Statistical assertions for validating patterns and finding bugs in quantum programs," in *Proceedings of the 46th International Symposium on Computer Architecture*, 2019, pp. 541–553.
[43] F. Leymann and J. Barzen, *Pattern Atlas*. Springer International Publishing, Apr. 2021, pp. 67–76.
[44] PlanQK, "PlanQK - Pattern Atlas," https://patterns.platform.planqk.de/pattern-languages, [accessed: 2023.05.25].
[45] M. Weigold *et al.*, "Pattern Views: Concept and Tooling of Interconnected Pattern Languages," in *Proceedings of the 14th Symposium and Summer School on Service-Oriented Computing (SummerSOC 2020)*. Springer International Publishing, Dec. 2020, pp. 86–103.
[46] P. Sánchez and D. Alonso, "On the Definition of Quantum Programming Modules," *Applied Sciences*, vol. 11, no. 13, 5843, 2021.
[47] PlanQK, "PlanQK - Platform and Ecosystem for Quantum Applications," https://platform.planqk.de/, [accessed: 2023.05.25].
[48] M. Falkenthal, J. Barzen, U. Breitenbücher, and F. Leymann, "Solution Languages: Easing Pattern Composition in Different Domains," *International Journal on Advances in Software*, vol. 10, no. 3, pp. 263–274, Dec. 2017.

Early Forecasting of At-Risk Students of Failing or Dropping Out of a Bachelor's Course Given Their Academic History - The Case Study of Numerical Methods

Isaac Caicedo-Castro[1 2 3], Mario Macea-Anaya[2 3 4], Samir Castaño-Rivera[1 3]
[1]*Socrates Research Team*
[2]*Research Team: Development, Education, and Healthcare*
[3]*Faculty of Engineering*
[4]*CINTIA, Center of INnovation in Technology of Information to support the Academia*
University of Córdoba
Carrera 6 No. 76-103, 230002, Montería, Colombia
emails: {isacaic, mariomacea, sacastano}@correo.unicordoba.edu.co

***Abstract*—In this work, we ponder the following research question: Is it possible to predict if a given student might either fail or drop out of an undergraduate course taking into account its performance in prerequisite courses? Therefore, we study the case of forecasting the risk faced by students of failing or dropping out of the course of numerical methods in an engineering bachelor's program. To this end, the prediction is based on the student's academic history, which consists of the grades the student has obtained in previous prerequisite courses, whose concepts and skills are required to succeed in the studied case of the numerical methods course. Additionally, the admission test results are also used for forecasting purposes. Moreover, we adopt machine learning, where supervised methods for classification are fitted using the academic history of students enrolled in the Engineering bachelor's program with a major in Systems Engineering at the University of Córdoba in Colombia. We collected the academic history of 56 anonymized students and carried out 10-fold cross-validation. The results of this study reveal that a support vector machines method predicts if a given student is at risk of failing or withdrawing from the numerical methods course with mean values for accuracy, precision, recall, and harmonic mean (F_1) of 76.67%, 71.67%, 51.67%, and 57.67%, respectively. This method outperforms the others studied in this work.**

Keywords*—Machine learning; educational data mining; classification algorithm; dropout and failure forecasting; student long-term retention.

I. INTRODUCTION

This work is part of a broader project called Course Prophet, whose goal is to design and implement an intelligence system that predicts if a student is at risk of failing or dropping a bachelor's course, that belongs to the scientific computing area in engineering, such as, e.g., numerical methods, linear programming, and so forth. Therefore, in this work, we have studied the case of forecasting if a given student might fail or withdraw from the numerical methods course in the context of a bachelor's program with a major in systems engineering at the University of Córdoba in Colombia.

The problem coped in this work shall be defined in Section I-A, whilst we shall discuss the motivation to solve it in Section I-B. In Section I-C, we shall present the key assumptions taken into account in this study, and its scope. Furthermore, we shall outline the contributions and organization of the remainder of this paper in Section I-D.

A. Problem statement

In a bachelor's degree, courses are organized and grouped into each semester to train students. The foundation of each subject is typically covered in the first semesters, with more advanced topics introduced in the later semesters. This gradual progression enables students to acquire skills and knowledge progressively, starting with the basic concepts and building towards more elaborated theories. However, students may still find the coursework challenging at times, and instructors need to ensure that they do not become overwhelmed, to ensure a positive learning experience. So, some courses are prerequisites of more advanced ones, for instance, differential calculus is required to understand linear and non-linear programming. Therefore, it is expected that the student's performance in a given course is influenced by their performance in prerequisite courses. For example, a student who struggled to pass differential calculus might have poor performance in differential equations and numerical methods.

Considering the relationship between courses, we ponder the following research question: Can an artificial intelligence system learn the regular patterns in a student's academic history to predict whether the student is at risk of failing or withdrawing from a course, based on their academic performance in the prerequisite courses?

To answer this question, we studied the case of the numerical methods course, which builds on concepts taught in prerequisite courses like calculus, physics, and computer programming. This case study focused on the context of the engineering students at the University of Córdoba in Colombia, a public university.

To determine a student's risk of failing or withdrawing from the numerical methods course, we analysed their performance in these prerequisite courses. In addition, we also considered their performance in the Saber 11 test, which is the standardized test used for bachelor program admission in Colombia. In the United States, a similar test called the Scholastic

Assessment Test (SAT) is used for the same purpose. The University of Córdoba admits or rejects candidates based on their Saber 11 test scores.

The performance in prerequisite courses is measured through the student's grades, whilst the admission test scores achieved by the student, measure their proficiency in every subject evaluated in the Saber 11 test. Therefore the student's grades and Saber 11 scores are the independent variables or the student's features, whereas the failure or dropout risk is the target variable (a.k.a., dependent variable), hence, the problem is finding the functional dependency between independent variables and the target variable. In the particular context of this study, the artificial intelligence system must infer the regular patterns between the risk of failing or withdrawing from the numerical methods course and the grades and Saber 11 scores achieved by the students in the past.

B. Motivation

Bachelor students at Colombian universities are graded in the range from 0 up to 5. To maintain their student status, bachelor students at Colombian universities must achieve a minimum global average grade. At the University of Córdoba, students are required to maintain a global average grade of at least 3.3, as specified in Article 16 of the university's student code [1]. Article 28-th of the university's code states that if a student's global average grade is between 3 and 3.3, they must increase their grade to at least 3.3 in the next semester or risk being dropped out. If a student's grade falls below 3, they are automatically withdrawn from the university (cf., article 16-th in the student's code [1]). The student who fails courses might lose their student status according to university rules. This problem is commonly referred to as *student dropout*.

On the other hand, those students who dropout courses might take longer to fulfil the requirements to receive their bachelor's degree. This problem is known as *long-term retention*. Both issues might cause students psychological issues, frustration, and financial loss.

Identifying students at risk in advance, allows professors and lecturers to run plans of action and strategies to handle previously mentioned issues. Moreover, precautions may be taken to prevent those students from failing or withdrawing from their courses. Some strategies include psychological support for students, or professors might suggest books, papers, or websites, amongst other educative resources, which students at risk might consult to review the material required to succeed in the course.

Thus, eventually, students' dropout and long-term retention rates might decrease, considering that both problems are a serious concern in the higher education systems and for policy-making stakeholders at universities [2].

C. Key Assumptions and Limitations

In this study we have taken into account the following assumptions:

- In the context of this study, we assumed that to succeed in Numerical Methods course, the prerequisites are Linear Algebra, Calculus I, II, III, Physics I, II, III, Introduction to Computer Programming, Computer Programming I, II, and III. The subjects included in the Numerical Methods course are as follows:
  (i) Approximations and computer arithmetic: the concepts to understands these subjects are taught in Introduction to Computer Programming.
  (ii) Non-linear equations: students must have a working knowledge of integral calculus (taught in Calculus II), be able to program computers using iterative and selective control structures (skills taught in both Introduction to Computer Programming and Computer Programming I), and understand Taylor series, which is the foundation of the secant method, a numerical method used to solve non-linear equations.
  (iii) Systems of linear equations: the student must be familiar with matrix and vector operations taught in linear algebra in order to understand numerical methods such as, e.g., Gauss-Seidel or Jacobi. Besides, programming such methods are subjects dealt in computer programming II course.
  (iv) Interpolation: the student must know the topics taught in calculus II to understand the background of the Taylor polynomial interpolation, and the subjects taught in courses such as linear algebra, computer programming I, and II to implement the other numerical methods for interpolation.
  (v) Numerical integration: in this subject, algorithms are used for computing integrals which cannot be solved through analytic methods, hence, the student must know what integration is (taught in calculus II course), and how to calculate some integrals to understand this subject.
  (vi) Ordinary differential equations: In this subject, the student must know concepts from all prior mathematics courses. It would be appropriate if the student would have attended a differential equation course, however, in the context of this study, this course is simultaneously scheduled with numerical methods, so students attend both in the same semester.
  (vii) Numerical optimization: this subject is an introduction for more advanced courses such as, e.g., statistics, linear and non-linear programming, stochastic methods courses, and machine learning. To understand this subject, the student must have mastered topics taught in courses, such as computer programming II and III, linear algebra, basic calculus, and vector calculus (which is taught in calculus III course).
- We assumed that a given students is at risk as long as they might either fail or dropout the numerical methods course.
- We assumed the admission test called Saber 11 might

be useful to forecast the failure or dropout risk. As a consequence, the score in each evaluated area is an input variable for the prediction.

- We assumed that the student's grades in prerequisite courses and the score in the admission test are sufficient input variables for forecasting the failure or dropout risk.

The scope of the research is limited as follows:

- We did not aim at designing an artificial intelligence system that predicts the dropout rate nor the failure rate of a given course.
- We did not consider additional input variables for the prediction, such as, e.g., gender, ethnicity, or economic variables, because the students who took the survey are alike regarding these features. Thus, these features do not help to differentiate students contributing little information to the forecasting process. For instance, Figure 1 shows that 83.95% of the students in the sample are male. Figure 2 indicates that over 90% of the students do not consider themselves part of an ethnic group. Additionally, Figure 3 reveals that more than 80% of the students belong to the first economical stratum. This aligns with the information presented in Figure 4, where over 90% of the students' family incomes are lower than two monthly minimum wages.

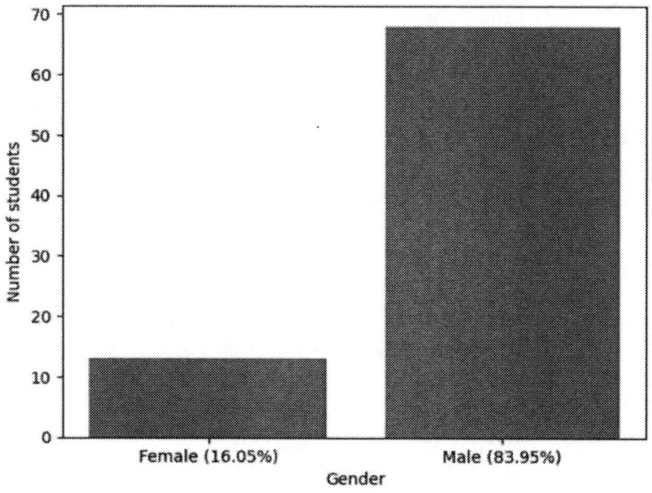

Figure 1. Sample distribution according to the students' gender.

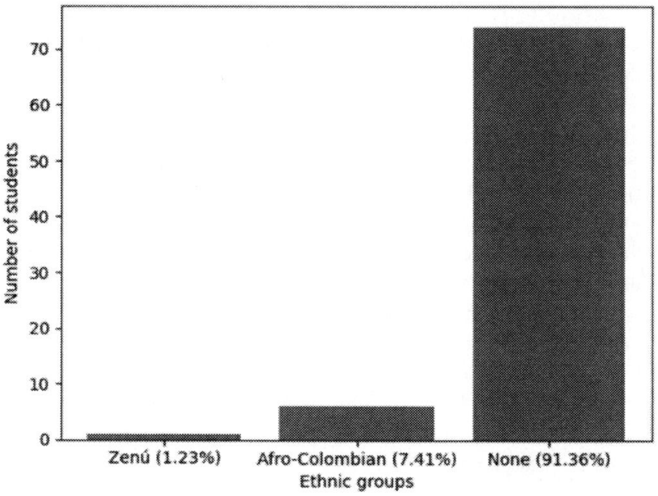

Figure 2. Sample distribution according to the students' ethnic group.

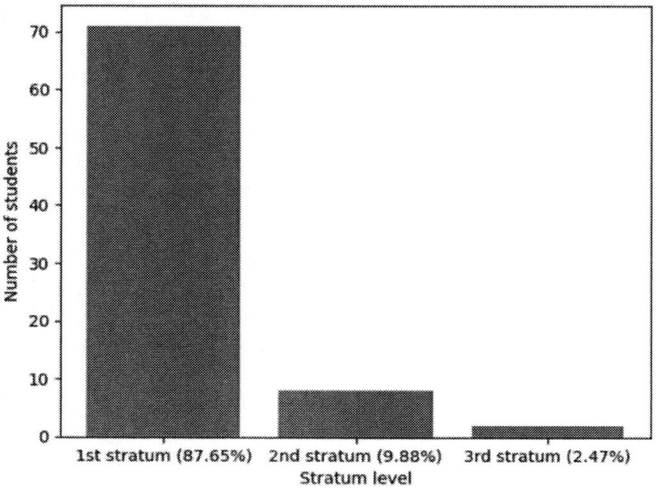

Figure 3. Sample distribution according to the students' economic stratification.

D. Contributions and Paper Outline

The contributions of this work are as follows:

(i) A dataset with 56 records, each one with 38 attributes corresponding to the independent variables, and another attribute, which is the target variable. These students have attended courses from the fifth semester up to the ninth semester during the second half of 2022.

(ii) The prototype of an intelligence system that learns regular patterns from the students' academic history to predict if a student might fail or dropout the numerical methods course.

(iii) An empirical study that reveals the support vector machine outperforms decision trees, Gaussian processes, artificial neural networks, amongst other machine learning methods. During the evaluation, the support vector machines achieved the mean values for accuracy, precision, recall, and harmonic mean (F_1) of 76.67%, 71.67%, 51.67%, and 57.67%, respectively.

The rest of this paper is outlined as follows: in Section II, we shall discuss the prior research on the problem addressed in this work, whilst we present the methods adopted in this study in Section III. In Section IV, we shall delve into de details of experimental setting, present and analyse the results. Finally, we shall draw the conclusions of this study and describe directions for further work in Section V.

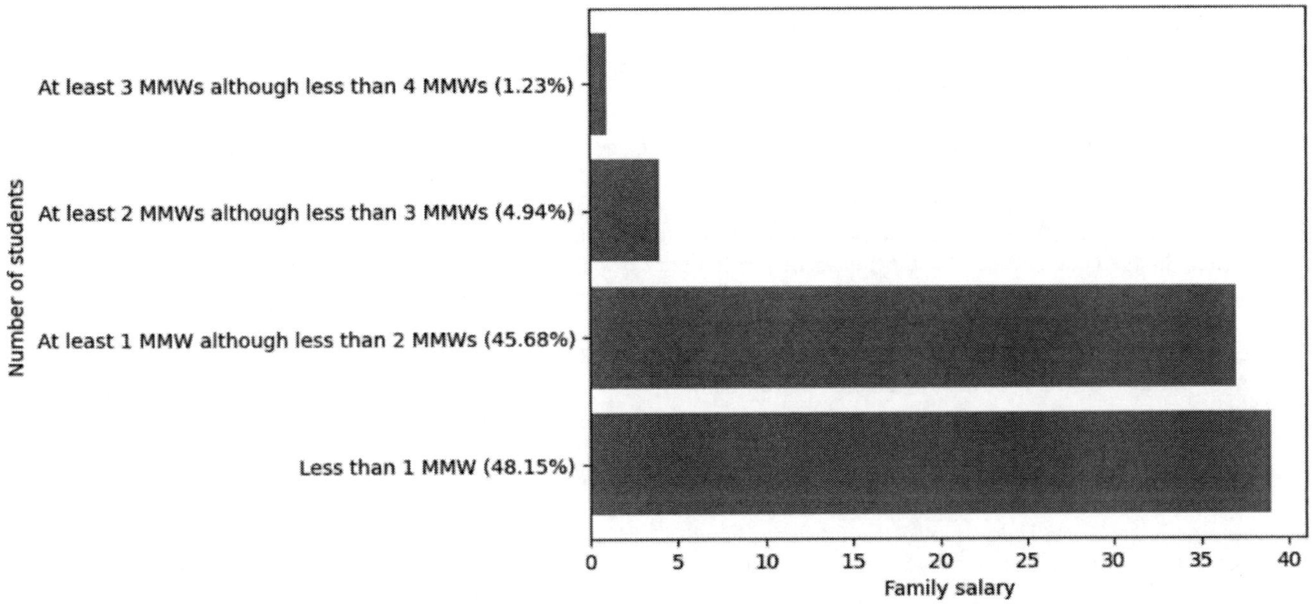

Figure 4. Sample distribution according to the students' family incomes in terms of Monthly Minimum Wages (MMW).

II. Related Work

This work falls within the domain of educational data mining, which aims to apply machine learning methods to large educational datasets to gain insights into students' learning behaviour. This includes analysing educational data, studying pedagogical theories using data mining, understanding students' domain knowledge, and evaluating their engagement in learning tasks.

Although course failure and dropout are general education problems, they have been mainly studied in the context of online education where predicting student dropout is a concerning issue. Previous research has used machine learning methods to forecast whether a given student will drop out of specific online courses, such as Computer Networks and Communications, and Web Design [3]. In contrast, our study aims not only to predict dropout but also to forecast the risk of failing a course. Additionally, our system aims to make predictions before the student begins the course, whilst the previously mentioned study has focused on predicting dropout during the course development.

Other studies have also focused on predicting failure and dropout risk, but they have used different independent variables compared to those in our study. For example, some studies have used the number of course views and scores achieved in assignments, tests, and projects as independent variables [4]. Other studies have used variables such as academic year, in addition to the aforementioned variables and others [5].

Only academic data, such as, e.g., students' age and grades have been used for predicting students dropout as well. However, grades have been considered ordinal data in lieu of quantitative information in some studies [6].

More recent studies conducted in the context of online courses have focused on the prediction of course dropout risk in STEM (Science, Technology, Engineering, and Mathematics) oriented courses [7] and mathematics course [8]. These studies use various independent variables, including the number of content downloads, scores obtained on weekly quizzes, video lesson views, and overall student activity in the course. The target variable is the course dropout risk.

It is important to note that in both of the latter related works, the prediction of the risk of not completing the course is primarily based on the student's behaviour during the learning process. Nevertheless, our study takes a different approach by focusing on the performance of the student in previous courses.

Additionally, other study is focused on predicting dropout from bachelor's degree instead of a specific course [9].

Furthermore, in the above-mentioned related works, the following machine learning classifiers have been adopted: artificial neural networks or multilayer perceptrons [3]–[6], [8], support vector machines [3], [4], [9], logistic regression [4], [7], [9], decision trees [4], [7], [9], ensemble methods with different kind of classifiers [3], [5], random forest [4]–[6], gradient boosting [6], XGBoost [5], [6], and variants of gradient boosting [6], [9], namely CatBoost [10] and LightGBM [11].

Finally, as far as we know, no related work has focused on the independent variables that we consider in this work, which are based on prerequisite student performance. Our aim is to predict the risk of failure or dropout for a specific course.

III. Methods

In this work, we adopted a quantitative approach, using students' grades that measure the performance during their academic history, including their scores achieved in the admission test known as Saber 11. Moreover, due to we used machine learning methods for forecasting, this work is also experimental regarding the nature of this approach, i.e., machine learning is an empirical discipline. With the experimental work, our goal is measuring the quality of the forecasting that depends on the capability of the machine learning methods to generalize properly with new input data.

In order to fit the machine learning methods, it is necessary to collect a dataset that include the history of students who have failed, dropped out and succeeded the numerical methods course, including their performance in the prerequisite courses and admission test. The machine learning methods capture the regular patterns that let the intelligence system predict the target variable given new input variables corresponding to future students.

The remainder of this section is organized as follows: we shall explain the procedure carried out to collect the dataset in Section III-A. In Section III-B, we shall discuss about the machine learning methods adopted in this study. Finally, in Section III-C, we shall describe the evaluation approach conducted in this work.

A. The Dataset Collection

In 2022, we conducted a survey on 81 students pursuing the bachelor's degree of engineering with major in systems engineering at the University of Córdoba in Colombia. These students have attended courses from the fifth semester up to the ninth semester.

In 2018, the curriculum structure of the above-mentioned bachelor's changed, thereby, we dropped 25 records corresponding to those students who started to pursue the bachelor's degree with the previous curriculum structure. Therefore the resulting dataset contains 56 out of 81 original records.

Let $\mathcal{D} = \{(\mathbf{x}_i, y_i) | \mathbf{x}_i \in \mathbb{R}^D \wedge y_i \in \{0,1\} \forall i = 1, 2, \ldots n\}$ be the complete dataset, where D and n are the number of independent variables and records, respectively. If the ith student either failed or dropped out the numerical method course, the target variable is equal to one, i.e., $y_i = 1$, otherwise it is equal to zero, i.e., $y_i = 0$. The real-valued $\mathbf{x}_i$ represents the ith student's record, and its components represent the independent variables. The first five components are scores achieved by a given student in each subject evaluated through the admission test called Saber 11, and each score is in the range of 0 up to 100, i.e., $x_{ij} \in \mathbb{Z}$, where $0 \leq x_{ij} \leq 100$ for $j = 1, 2, \ldots, 5$. On the other hand, for each prerequisite course, there are components whose values are the student's highest and lowest grade, including the number of semesters the student has attended the course. Each grade is a real-valued number between 0 and 5. There are eleven prerequisite courses, hence, there are thirty three components, besides the previous five ones, thereby, there is a total of 38 components in every vector, i.e., $D = 38$. The meaning of each component is explained as follows:

- x_{i1} is the score achieved by the ith student in the mathematics subject of the admission test.
- x_{i2} is the score achieved by the ith student in the natural science subject of the admission test.
- x_{i3} is the score achieved by the ith student in the social science subject of the admission test.
- x_{i4} is the score achieved by the ith student in the critical reading subject of the admission test.
- x_{i5} is the score achieved by the ith student in the social English proficiency evaluation of the admission test.
- x_{i6} is the best grade that a given student achieved in Calculus I course.
- x_{i7} is the number of semester a given student has attended the Calculus I course.
- x_{i8} is the worst that a given student achieved in Calculus I course.
- x_{i9} is the best grade that a given student achieved in Calculus II course.
- $x_{i,10}$ is the number of semester a given student has attended the Calculus II course.
- $x_{i,11}$ is the worst that a given student achieved in Calculus II course.
- $x_{i,12}$ is the best grade that a given student achieved in Calculus III course.
- $x_{i,13}$ is the number of semester a given student has attended the calculus III course.
- $x_{i,14}$ is the worst that a given student achieved in Calculus III course.
- $x_{i,15}$ is the best grade that a given student achieved in Linear Algebra course.
- $x_{i,16}$ is the number of semester a given student has attended the Linear Algebra course.
- $x_{i,17}$ is the worst that a given student achieved in Linear Algebra course.
- $x_{i,18}$ is the best grade that a given student achieved in Physics I course.
- $x_{i,19}$ is the number of semester a given student has attended the Physics I course.
- $x_{i,20}$ is the worst that a given student achieved in Physics I course.
- $x_{i,21}$ is the best grade that a given student achieved in Physics II course.
- $x_{i,22}$ is the number of semester a given student has attended the Physics II course.
- $x_{i,23}$ is the worst that a given student achieved in Physics II course.
- $x_{i,24}$ is the best grade that a given student achieved in Physics III course.
- $x_{i,25}$ is the number of semester a given student has attended the Physics III course.
- $x_{i,26}$ is the worst that a given student achieved in Physics III course.
- $x_{i,27}$ is the best grade that a given student achieved in Introduction to Computer Programming course.
- $x_{i,28}$ is the number of semester a given student has attended the Introduction to Computer Programming course.
- $x_{i,29}$ is the worst that a given student achieved in Introduction to Computer Programming course.
- $x_{i,30}$ is the best grade that a given student achieved in

Computer Programming I course.

- $x_{i,31}$ is the number of semester a given student has attended the Computer Programming I course.
- $x_{i,32}$ is the worst that a given student achieved in Computer Programming I course.
- $x_{i,33}$ is the best grade that a given student achieved in Computer Programming II course.
- $x_{i,34}$ is the number of semester a given student has attended the Computer Programming II course.
- $x_{i,35}$ is the worst that a given student achieved in Computer Programming II course.
- $x_{i,36}$ is the best grade that a given student achieved in Computer Programming III course.
- $x_{i,37}$ is the number of semester a given student has attended the Computer Programming III course.
- $x_{i,38}$ is the worst that a given student achieved in Computer Programming III course.

The dataset is not utterly balanced, nevertheless, Figure 5 shows it contains enough positive examples, namely those where the students have either failed or dropped out courses.

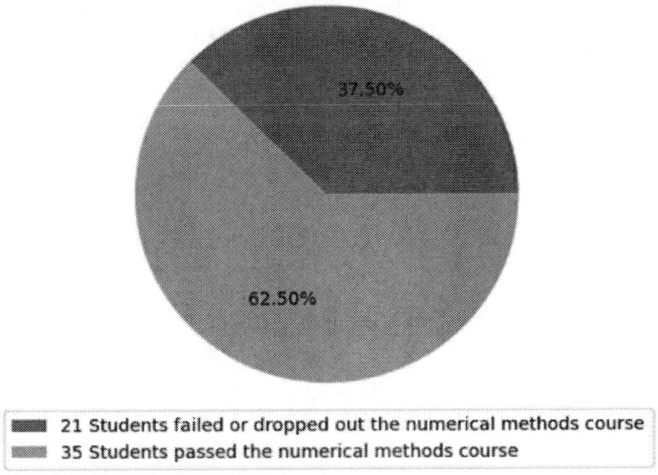

Figure 5. Distribution of students who have failed or dropped out the numerical course in compared to those ones who passed it

B. Classification Methods

The problem addressed in this work is finding the functional dependency between the independent variables, $\mathbf{x} \in \mathbb{R}^D$, and the target variable, $y \in \{0, 1\}$, in other words, fitting the function $f : \mathbb{R}^D \rightarrow \{0, 1\}$ given the training dataset (which is a portion of the whole dataset). To cope this problem we adopted supervised learning approach, specifically, classification methods.

We used logistic regression as our first classification method to predict the probability between two possible outcomes. Logistic regression utilizes the sigmoid function of the linear combination between input variables and weights, which are fitted by maximizing the objective function based on the log-likelihood of the training data given the binary outcome [12]. We fitted the logistic regression classifier through Limited-memory Broyden-Fletcher-Goldfarb-Shanno (L-BFGS) algorithm [13], [14].

With the logistic regression method, it is assumed there exists a discriminant hyperplane to separate the examples in two classes, which might be a reasonable assumption regarding the high dimensionality of the dataset used in this study. Nevertheless, we also adopted other classifiers that are far better suited for non-linear classification problems, such as the Gaussian process classifier. This is a probabilistic method based on Bayesian inference. In the Gaussian process, the probability distribution of the target variable is Gaussian or normal, this explains the name of the method [15], [16]. The main advantage of the Gaussian process classifier is the possibility of incorporating prior knowledge about the problem, improving its forecasting even when the training dataset is small. However, the computational cost of fitting and making predictions with this method can become an issue in domains with large-scaled datasets. In the context of this study, the dataset is rather small, which makes the Gaussian process classifier a suitable choice.

So far, the support vector machines (SVM) method is the best theoretical motivated and one of the most successful methods in the practice of modern machine learning [17, pg. 79]. It is based on convex optimization, allowing for a global maximum solution to be found, which is its main advantage. However, SVM method is not well-suited for interpretation in data mining and is better suited for training accurate intelligent systems. A broader description of this algorithm can be found in the work by Cortes and Vapnik [18].

Both SVM and logistic regression are linear classification methods that assume the input vector space can be separated by a linear decision boundary (or a hyperplane in the case of a multidimensional space). However, when this assumption is not satisfied, SVM can be used with kernel methods to handle non-linear decision boundaries (see Cortes and Vapnik [18] for further details).

Although SVM method is considered one of the most successful methods in the practice of modern machine learning, multilayer perceptrons and their variants, which are artificial neural networks, are the most successful methods in the practice of deep learning and big data, particularly in tasks such as speech recognition, computer vision, natural language processing, and so forth. [19, pg. 3]. In this research, we have adopted the multilayer perceptrons fitted through back-propagated cross-entropy error [20], and the optimization algorithm known as Adam [21]. We used multilayer perceptrons with one and five hidden layers.

The multilayer perceptron method is a universal approximator (i.e., it is able to approximate any function for either classification or regression), which is its main advantage. However, its main disadvantage is that the objective function (a.k.a., loss function) based on the cross-entropy error is not convex. Therefore, the synaptic weights obtained through the fitting process might not converge to the most optimum solution because there are several local minima in the objective function. Thus, finding a solution depends on the random initialization of the synaptic weights. Furthermore, multilayer perceptrons have more hyperparameters to be tuned than other learning algorithms (e.g., support vector machines or naive Bayes), which is an additional shortcoming.

Except for the logistic regression method, all the above-mentioned methods are not easily interpretable. Therefore, we adopted decision trees, which are classification algorithms commonly used in data mining and knowledge discovery. In decision tree training, a tree is created using the dataset as input, where each internal node represents a test on an independent variable, each branch represents the result of the test, and leaves represent forecasted classes. The construction of the tree is carried out in a recursive way, beginning with the whole dataset as the root node, and at each iteration, the fitting algorithm selects the next attribute that best separates the data into different classes. The fitting algorithm can be stopped based on several criteria, such as when all the training data is classified or when the accuracy or performance of the classifier cannot be further improved.

Decision trees are fitted through heuristic algorithms, such as greedy algorithms, which may lead to several local optimal solutions at each node. This is one of the reasons why there is no guarantee that the learning algorithm will converge to the most optimal solution, as is also the case with the multilayer perceptrons algorithm. Therefore, this is the main drawback of decision trees, and it can cause completely different tree shapes due to small variations in the training dataset. The decision trees were proposed in 1984, Breiman *et al.* delve into their details (cf., [22]). We also adopted ensemble methods based on multiple decision trees such as, e.g., Adaboost (stands for adaptive boosting) [23], Random forest [24], and XGBoost [25].

C. Evaluation Approach

To evaluate the machine learning methods, we need several pairs of training and test datasets. To this end, we carried out experiments based on K-Fold Cross-Validation (KFCV), hence, from the original dataset, we get K pairs of training and test datasets. We chose $K = 10$, where it is usually 10 or 30. We did not choose $K = 30$ because the dataset is small. Thus, we test each method K times through KFCV. With the test outcomes, we calculate the mean accuracy, mean precision, and mean recall to compare the learning methods, and choosing the best hyper-parameters for each method (e.g., the regularization parameter in the multilayer perceptrons and logistic regression).

IV. Evaluation

Given the no free lunch theorem, there is no universal best machine learning method for the problem at hand. To identify the most effective method, we conducted an experiment using the models described in Section III-B. Details of the experimental setup can be found in Section IV-A, with results and their discussion presented in Sections IV-B and IV-C, respectively.

A. Experimental Setting

The evaluation is conducted through K-fold cross-validation, where K = 10, as it was mentioned in Section III-C. This procedure is preformed in a dataset that contains 56 records or examples, with 38 independent variables for each example (see Section III-A). The dataset is available online to allow the reproduction of our study, and for further research [26].

Finally, we programmed all the experiments with Python, using the Scikit-Learn library [27], in Google Colaboratory [28].

B. Results

The results of the 10-fold cross-validation evaluation are summarized in table I. Support vector machines (SVM) with radial basis function kernel outperforms the other classification methods in terms of accuracy and harmonic mean (F_1). Nonetheless, Random forest classifier achieved the highest precision, whilst the decision tree classification method reached the best recall.

The mean recall value of the SVM with radial basis is in line with the confusion matrix presented in Table II. During all iterations of the 10-fold cross-validation evaluation, the classifier correctly predicted only 11 out of 21 students at risk, resulting in almost half of the actual positive examples being falsely classified as negative (i.e., false negative instances). Conversely, the SVM classifier misclassified only three examples as positive, which aligns with the mean precision achieved during the evaluation. These results indicate that the classifier has a low probability of misclassifying students not at risk as being at risk, which is beneficial in avoiding the wastage of resources for students who do not need them. However, this classifier might miss identifying some students who are actually at risk. The decision tree with entropy index outperformed the recall of others classifiers, nevertheless, the mean recall difference between the decision tree and SVM is not statistically significant (i.e., p-value > 0.05), as it is shown in Table I.

Regarding the size of the dataset, Figure 6 shows the receiver operating characteristics (ROC) curve for the SVM with radial basis function kernel. The area under the curve (AUC) of 0.68 indicates that the classifier performs better than random guessing, or that it provides some level of discrimination between positive and negative examples. However, a larger dataset might improve this performance. It is worth noting that the AUC of this classifier is lower than the AUC of the classifiers shown in Figure 7. In particular, random forest outperforms the other classification methods in distinguishing between positive and negative examples, with an AUC of 0.77.

In the domain of this study, where we are interesting in predicting students at risk, it might be more important a classification method that forecasts accurately to either avoid spend resources in students who do not require them, or to not help students who actually might fail or dropout the numerical methods course. In other domains, such as, e.g.,

TABLE I
TEN-FOLD CROSS-VALIDATION RESULTS

Machine learning method	*Mean Accuracy (%)*	*p-value*	*Mean Precision (%)*	*p-value*	*Mean Recall (%)*	*p-value*	*Mean* $\mathbf{F_1}$ *(%)*	*p-value*
Support vector machines with the radial basis function kernel	**76.67**		71.67		51.67		**57.67**	
Support vector machines with the sigmoid kernel	71.67	0.45	40	0.15	23.33	0.08	28.33	0.08
Support vector machines with the polynomial kernel (degree = 3)	66.67	2.26	48.33	0.22	48.33	0.84	46.67	0.51
Decision tree with entropy index	68.33	0.34	48.33	0.18	**70**	0.3	56.57	0.94
Decision tree with gini index	62.33	0.11	47.5	0.18	56.67	0.76	50	0.61
Logistic regression	64	0.1	47.5	0.24	28.33	0.09	33.33	0.1
Multilayer perceptron with a single hidden layer	57	**0.005**†	18.33	**0.006**†	25	0.1	20	**0.01**†
Multilayer perceptron with five hidden layers	64.33	**0.04**†	6.67	**0.0003**†	10	**0.01**†	8	**0.001**†
Gaussian process with the rational quadratic kernel	68.67	0.31	50	0.32	28.33	0.14	35	0.17
Gaussian process with the periodic kernel	62.33	**0.01**†	0	$\mathbf{3.57 \times 10^{-5}}$†	0	$\mathbf{1.3 \times 10^{-4}}$†	0	$\mathbf{3.05 \times 10^{-5}}$†
Gaussian process with the dot product kernel	62.33	**0.04**†	43.33	0.12	43.33	0.61	39.67	0.21
Gaussian process with the Matern kernel	69.67	0.32	65	0.72	38.33	0.3	38.33	0.45
Gaussian process with the radial basis function kernel	73.33	0.66	70	0.93	48.33	0.82	53.67	0.78
Gaussian process with a sum of radial basis function and Matern kernel	70	0.4	63.33	0.68	38.33	0.37	45.67	0.44
Random forest with the entropy index	72	0.56	**75.83**	0.82	48.33	0.8	55.67	0.88
Adaboost with the entropy index	66.33	0.23	46.67	0.15	65	0.43	53.57	0.79
XGBoost	61	0.08	45.83	0.18	38.33	0.37	39.67	0.24

†Student's paired t-test reveals the difference between means is statistically significant

TABLE II
CONFUSION MATRIX FOR SUPPORT VECTOR MACHINES WITH RADIAL BASIS FUNCTION

	Forecasted class		
True class	*Student without risk*	*Student at risk*	*Total*
Student without risk	32	3	35
Student at risk	10	11	21
Total	42	14	56

fraud detection, it might be far more useful a classifier with high AUC to minimize false positives.

Furthermore, the best hyper-parameter setting for each approach, corresponding with the results shown in table I, is presented as follows:

- Gaussian process classifier with radial basis function kernel, the best values for σ and γ are 4 and 8, respectively, where both values are applied to the formula $k_G(\mathbf{x}_i, \mathbf{x}_j) = \gamma \exp(-||\mathbf{x}_j - \mathbf{x}_i||^2 / 2\sigma^2)$.
- Gaussian process classifier with Matern kernel, the best values for nu, σ and γ are 1.5, 3 and 1.5×10^{-5}, respectively, where these values are applied to the formula $k_M(\mathbf{x}_i, \mathbf{x}_j) = \gamma \frac{1}{\Gamma(\nu) 2^{\nu-1}} \big(\frac{\sqrt{2\nu}||\mathbf{x}_j - \mathbf{x}_i||^2}{\sigma}\big)^\nu K_\nu\big(\frac{\sqrt{2\nu}||\mathbf{x}_j - \mathbf{x}_i||^2}{\sigma}\big)$, where $K_\nu(\cdot)$ and $\Gamma(\cdot)$ are the modified Bessel function and the

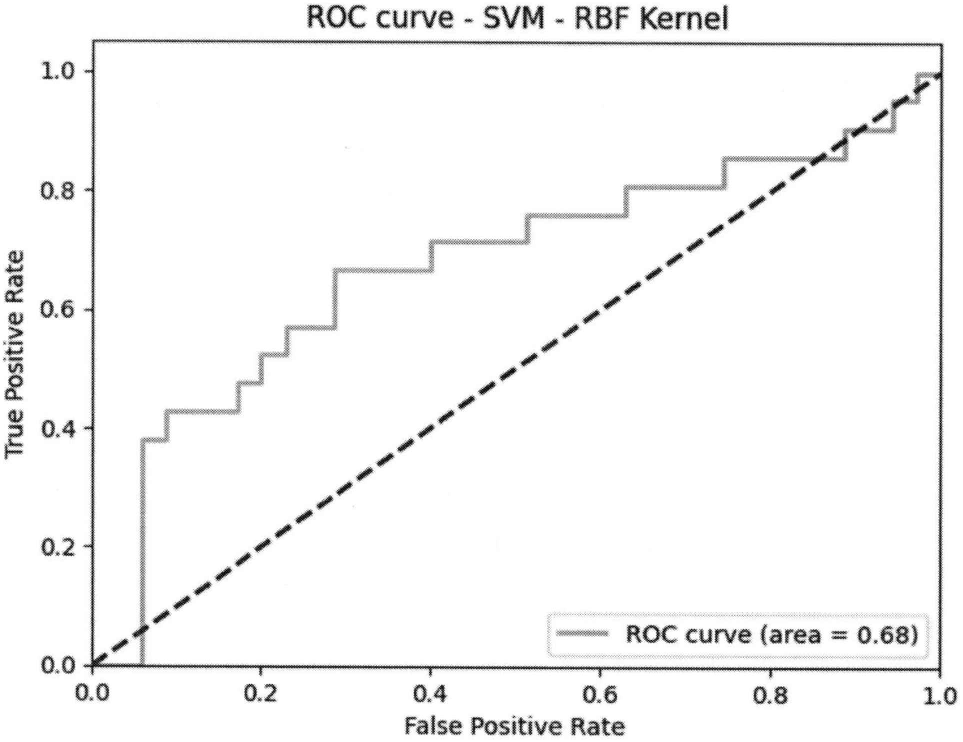

Figure 6. The ROC curve for support vector machine with radial basis function kernel

gamma function, respectively.

- Gaussian process classifier with the combination between radial basis function and Matern kernel as follows: $k(\mathbf{x}_i, \mathbf{x}_j) = \gamma_G k_G(\mathbf{x}_i, \mathbf{x}_j) + \gamma_M k_M(\mathbf{x}_i, \mathbf{x}_j)$, where γ_G and γ_M are 8 and 1.5×10^{-5}, respectively. The hyper-parameter values used in the two previous kernels are also used in this combination.
- Gaussian process classifier with dot product kernel, which is defined a follows: $k_d(\mathbf{x}_i, \mathbf{x}_j) = 1 + \langle \mathbf{x}_i, \mathbf{x}_j \rangle$.
- Gaussian process classifier with periodic kernel, where $sigma$ and p (periodicity) are 2^{-16} and 3, respectively. The periodic kernel is defined as follows: $k_p(\mathbf{x}_i, \mathbf{x}_j) = \exp\left(-\frac{2\sin^2(\pi||\mathbf{x}_j - \mathbf{x}_i||^2/p)}{\sigma^2}\right)$.
- Gaussian process classifier with rational quadratic kernel, where σ and α are both 3×10^5. The kernel is defined as follows: $k_r(\mathbf{x}_i, \mathbf{x}_j) = (1 + ||\mathbf{x}_j - \mathbf{x}_i||^2/(2\alpha\sigma^2))^{-\alpha}$
- SVM with radial basis function kernel, where γ and C are 3.9×10^{-3} and 2, respectively. In this case the kernel is defined as follows: $k_G(\mathbf{x}_i, \mathbf{x}_j) = \exp(-\gamma||\mathbf{x}_j - \mathbf{x}_i||^2)$.
- SVM with polynomial kernel, where d (degree) and C are 3 and 4096, respectively. The kernel is defined as follows: $k_p(\mathbf{x}_i, \mathbf{x}_j) = \langle \mathbf{x}_i, \mathbf{x}_j \rangle^d$.
- SVM with sigmoid kernel, where γ and C are 4.88×10^{-4} and 32768, respectively. The kernel is defined as follows: $k_s(\mathbf{x}_i, \mathbf{x}_j) = \tanh \gamma \langle \mathbf{x}_i, \mathbf{x}_j \rangle$.
- Multilayer perceptron with a single hidden layer, with 600 neurons in the hidden layer. This was fitted with an initial learning rate and regularization parameter equal to 10^{-4} and 10^{-2}, respectively. The activation function used in the hidden layer is hyperbolic tangent function.
- Multilayer perceptron with five hidden layers. The number of neurons in the first, second, third, fourth, and fifth layer are 600, 300, 100, 300, and 600, respectively. This was fitted with an initial learning rate and regularization parameter equal to 10^{-4} and 10^{-2}, respectively. The activation function used in the hidden layer is hyperbolic tangent function.
- Logistic regression classifier was fitted with a regularization parameter of 10^{-2}.
- The decision trees were fitted using both the Gini and entropy indexes. The parameters used were the given by default in Scikit-Learn API.
- XGBoost algorithm were fitted with a learning rate, maximum depth, and number of estimators equal to 3.13×10^{-2}, 5, and 50, respectively. Besides, we used the entropy index in the trees.
- Adaboost algorithm were fitted with a learning rate and number of estimators equal to 0.13 and 110, respectively. Besides, we used the entropy index in the trees.
- Random forest were fitted with 15 trees (with entropy index), at least one sample per leaf, minimum three samples per split, and a maximum depth of nine levels.

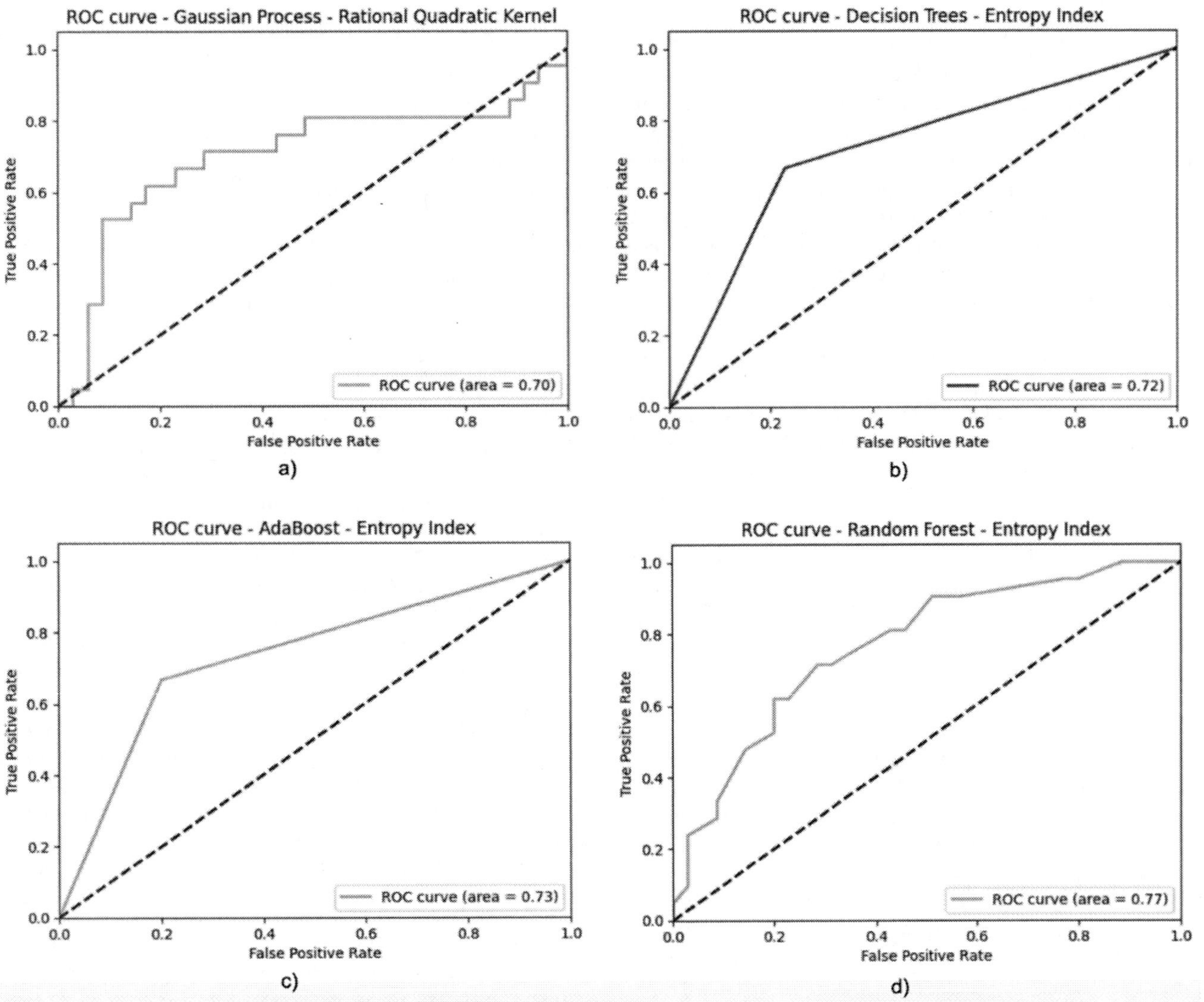

Figure 7. The ROC curve for a) Gaussian process classifier with Rational quadratic kernel, b) decision tree with entropy index, c) Adaboost, and d) random forest

C. Discussion

Based on the evaluation results, we found that the Support Vector Machines (SVM) method with radial basis function kernels was the most accurate classifier tested in this study. However, when we conducted a paired t-test, we found statistically significant evidence that SVM outperformed multilayer perceptrons and Gaussian processes with dot product and periodic kernels, but we did not find strong statistical evidence that SVM was more accurate than all the other classifiers.

In addition, the paired t-test showed that the harmonic mean (F_1) of SVM was significantly better than that of multilayer perceptrons and Gaussian process classifiers with the periodic kernel. However, we did not find strong statistical evidence for a significant difference between the harmonic mean of SVM and the other evaluated classifiers.

Moreover, we observed that the multilayer perceptron and the Gaussian process classifier with the periodic kernel had the poorest performance amongst the classifiers tested in this study. It is possible that increasing the dataset size might improve the performance of the multilayer perceptron. In contrast, the poor performance of the Gaussian process classifier with the periodic kernel might be due to the model's inability to repeat itself exactly.

Whilst the random forest classifier achieved the highest precision amongst the classifiers tested in this work, the paired t-test showed no significant difference between its precision and that of SVM with radial basis function kernels. However, random forest performed better than SVM in distinguishing between positive and negative examples, as evidenced by its higher area under the ROC curve (AUC) of 0.77, compared to SVM's AUC of 0.68. This difference is shown in Figures 6 and 7, and suggests that random forest is better at accurately identifying true positives and true negatives than SVM, even though SVM is slightly more accurate overall.

Furthermore, the decision trees that make up the random forest classifier can be used to extract insights and discover knowledge that can help formulate theories about how a student's performance in prerequisite courses might influence their performance in numerical methods. By analysing the tree structure and the features that lead to high or low performance, we can gain a better understanding of the underlying relationships between these variables and potentially develop new strategies for improving student outcomes.

The Gaussian process classifier with the radial basis function kernel is another strong candidate for classification, as it was the second most accurate method according to our results. One advantage of this classifier over SVM is that it provides a probability estimate of a given student being at risk, which can be useful for making decisions. In contrast, SVM method does not provide such a probability estimate.

To draw a more solid conclusion about the best classifier for this problem, we would need to collect additional data to evaluate the performance and generalization capability of the classifiers.

V. Conclusions and Future Work

In this work, we have studied several machine learning methods for forecasting if a given student is at risk of failing or withdrawing from the Numerical Methods course based on their performance in prerequisite courses.

The aforementioned study was conducted using a dataset with 56 records and 39 variables each (i.e., 38 independent variables and one target variable), collected from students who have attended courses from the fifth semester up to ninth semester during the second half of 2022. The findings of the study conducted in this work are as follows:

- Support vector machine (SVM) with the radial basis function is more accurate than the other studied methods, reaching the mean values for accuracy, precision, recall, and harmonic mean (F_1) of 76.67%, 71.67%, 51.67%, and 57.67%, respectively.
- Whilst there is no strong statistical evidence that SVM is more accurate than the other studied methods, there is solid evidence that SVM with the radial basis function outperforms the multilayer perceptron with one or several hidden layers, as well as the Gaussian process classifier with periodic and dot product kernels.
- SVM performs better with the radial basis function kernel than with polynomial and sigmoid kernels.
- Gaussian process (GP) performs better with the radial basis function kernel than with the other kernels evaluated in this study.
- GP with the radial basis function is the second classifier more accurate according to the evaluation conducted in this study.
- During the evaluation, Random forest (RF) was found to be the third more accurate classifier, with the highest mean recall amongst all methods.
- There is no statistically significant difference between the mean recall of RF and SVM with the radial basis function.

For further work we recommend:

- Collect more data to study the performance of some learning methods such as, e.g., multilayer perceptron, random forest, Adaboost, and so forth.
- Combine more kernels in the Gaussian processes to study their performance.
- Extend this study to other courses besides numerical methods.
- Analyse the decision trees generated by random forest, Adaboost, XGBoost, and other methods in more detail, with the aim of identifying patterns or rules that can help us gain deeper insights into the problem at hand.
- Propose a novel method that surpasses the performance of all previously studied methods in this work, achieving significantly higher accuracy and harmonic mean scores.
- Despite the dataset being sufficiently large, leading to improved performance of most classification methods compared to random guessing, with one of them achieving an area under the ROC curve (AUC) of 0.77, we shall collect a larger dataset for further research. By doing so, we might draw more robust conclusions regarding the performance of the classifiers.
- Investigate the effectiveness of strategies and precautions, such as, e.g., mentoring programs and personalized feedback, in coping with the risks of failure and dropout faced by students.

Acknowledgement

Caicedo-Castro thanks the Lord Jesus Christ for blessing this project. We thank Universidad de Córdoba in Colombia for supporting the Course Prophet Research Project (grant FI-01-22). In special, our deepest appreciation goes to Dr. Jairo Torres-Oviedo, rector of the University of Córdoba, who has always helped us and supported us throughout this research. We thank all students who collaborated with us, answering the survey conducted for collecting the dataset, used to train the learning algorithms adopted in this research. Finally, we thank the anonymous reviewers for their comments that contributed to improve the quality of this article.

References

[1] I. Pacheco-Arrieta *et al.* (2004) Agreement No. 004: Student's code at the University of Córdoba in Colombia. Retrieved on May 24. [Online]. Available: http://www.unicordoba.edu.co/wp-content/uploads/2018/12/reglamento-academico.pdf

[2] C. Demetriou and A. Schmitz-Sciborski, "Integration , Motivation , Strengths and Optimism : Retention Theories Past , Present and Future," in *Proceedings of the 7th National Symposium on Student Retention*, 2011, pp. 300–312.

[3] I. Lykourentzou, I. Giannoukos, V. Nikolopoulos, G. Mpardis, and V. Loumos, "Dropout prediction in e-learning courses through the combination of machine learning techniques," *Computers and Education*, vol. 53, no. 3, pp. 950–965, 2009.

[4] J. Kabathova and M. Drlik, "Towards Predicting Student's Dropout in University Courses Using Different Machine Learning Techniques," *Applied Sciences*, vol. 11, p. 3130, 04 2021.

[5] J. Niyogisubizo, L. Liao, E. Nziyumva, E. Murwanashyaka, and P. C. Nshimyumukiza, "Predicting student's dropout in university classes using two-layer ensemble machine learning approach: A novel stacked generalization," *Computers and Education: Artificial Intelligence*, vol. 3, p. 100066, 2022.

[6] D. E. M. da Silva, E. J. S. Pires, A. Reis, P. B. de Moura Oliveira, and J. Barroso, "Forecasting Students Dropout: A UTAD University Study," *Future Internet*, vol. 14, no. 3, pp. 1–14, February 2022.

[7] V. Čotić Poturić, I. Dražić, and S. Čandrlić, "Identification of Predictive Factors for Student Failure in STEM Oriented Course," in *ICERI2022 Proceedings*, ser. 15th annual International Conference of Education, Research and Innovation. IATED, 2022, pp. 5831–5837.

[8] V. Čotić Poturić, A. Bašić-Šiško, and I. Lulić, "Artificial neural network model for forecasting student failure in math course," in *ICERI2022 Proceedings*, ser. 15th annual International Conference of Education, Research and Innovation. IATED, 2022, pp. 5872–5878.

[9] S. Zihan, S.-H. Sung, D.-M. Park, and B.-K. Park, "All-Year Dropout Prediction Modeling and Analysis for University Students," *Applied Sciences*, vol. 13, p. 1143, 01 2023.

[10] A. V. Dorogush, V. Ershov, and A. Gulin, "CatBoost: gradient boosting with categorical features support," *CoRR*, vol. abs/1810.11363, 2018.

[11] G. Ke, Q. Meng, T. Finley, T. Wang, W. Chen, W. Ma, Q. Ye, and T.-Y. Liu, "LightGBM: A Highly Efficient Gradient Boosting Decision Tree," in *Advances in Neural Information Processing Systems*, I. Guyon, U. V. Luxburg, S. Bengio, H. Wallach, R. Fergus, S. Vishwanathan, and R. Garnett, Eds., vol. 30. Curran Associates, Inc., 2017.

[12] D. Cox, "The regression analysis of binary sequences," *Journal of the Royal Statistical Society. Series B (Methodological)*, vol. 20, no. 2, pp. 215–242, 1958.

[13] D. C. Liu and J. Nocedal, "On the limited memory BFGS method for large scale optimization," *Mathematical Programming*, vol. 45, no. 3, (Ser. B), pp. 503–528, 1989.

[14] R. Byrd, P. Lu, J. Nocedal, and C. Zhu, "A Limited Memory Algorithm for Bound Constrained Optimization," *SIAM Journal on Scientific Computing*, vol. 16, no. 5, pp. 1190–1208, 1995.

[15] C. Williams and C. Rasmussen, "Gaussian Processes for Regression," in *Advances in Neural Information Processing Systems*, D. Touretzky, M. Mozer, and M. Hasselmo, Eds., vol. 8. MIT Press, 1995, pp. 514–520.

[16] C. E. Rasmussen and C. K. I. Williams, *Gaussian Processes for Machine Learning*. MIT Press, 2006.

[17] M. Mohri, A. Rostamizadeh, and A. Talwalkar, *Foundations of Machine Learning*, 2nd ed. The MIT Press, 2018.

[18] C. Cortes and V. Vapnik, "Support Vector Networks," *Machine Learning*, vol. 20, pp. 273–297, 1995.

[19] C. C. Aggarwal, *Neural Networks and Deep Learning*. Springer, 2018.

[20] D. E. Rumelhart, G. E. Hinton, and R. J. Williams, "Learning Representations by Back-propagating Errors," *Nature*, vol. 323, no. 6088, pp. 533–536, 1986.

[21] D. P. Kingma and J. Ba. (2014) Adam: A method for stochastic optimization. Retrieved on May 25. [Online]. Available: http://arxiv.org/abs/1412.6980

[22] L. Breiman, J. H. Friedman, R. A. Olshen, and C. J. Stone, *Classification and Regression Trees*. Monterey, CA: Wadsworth and Brooks, 1984.

[23] Y. Freund and R. E. Schapire, "Experiments with a new boosting algorithm," in *ICML*, vol. 96, 1996, pp. 148–156.

[24] L. Breiman, "Random forests," in *Machine learning*, vol. 45, no. 1. Springer, 2001, pp. 5–32.

[25] T. Chen and C. Guestrin, "Xgboost: A scalable tree boosting system," in *Proceedings of the 22nd ACM SIGKDD international conference on knowledge discovery and data mining*. ACM, 2016, pp. 785–794.

[26] I. Caicedo-Castro. (2023) Dataset for Early Forecasting of At-Risk Students of Failing or Dropping Out of a Bachelor's Course Given Their Academic History - The Case Study of Numerical Methods. Retrieved on May 25. [Online]. Available: https://sites.google.com/correo.unicordoba.edu.co/isacaic/research

[27] F. Pedregosa *et al.*, "Scikit-learn: Machine Learning in Python," *Journal of Machine Learning Research*, vol. 12, pp. 2825–2830, 2011.

[28] (2017) Google Colaboratory. Retrieved on May 25. [Online]. Available: https://colab.research.google.com/

Spatiotemporal Modeling of Urban Sprawl Using Machine Learning and Satellite Data

Alexander Troussov, Dmitri Botvich, and Sergey Maruev
International laboratory for mathematical modeling of social networks,
RANEPA,
Moscow, Russia
e-mails: {troussov, dbotvich, maruev}@gmail.com

***Abstract*—The paper discusses the issues related to the use of machine learning in designing and creating predictive models of the territorial development of cities. Special attention is paid to models that use satellite data, which is the most easily accessible type of data and allows for the use of machine learning. The proposed provisions are based on the authors' current experience in developing an information system for forecasting the territorial development of cities based on remote sensing data of the Earth. A novel approach to developing predictive models of urban growth is presented, which is based on machine learning methods. The approach uses satellite data from the Defense Meteorological Satellite Program/Operational Linescan System and Visible Infrared Imaging Radiometer Suite/Day-Night Band for training. The corresponding machine learning optimization problem is presented and discussed.**

***Keywords*—Earth remote sensing; urbanization; evolutionary models of urban development; cellular automata; machine learning.**

I. Introduction

Existing computational models of urban evolution are too resource-consuming, and the validation of forecasting results is quite complicated. However, the growing flow of new data, primarily data from remote sensing of the Earth, enables the use of the 'Big Data' approach for both prediction and validation purposes. Remote sensing data have a high spatial resolution and global coverage and are collected according to a common methodology. To learn the model of a particular city (or agglomeration) development, one can use both historical data from a given city and data from other "similar" cities. The parameters of the computational model based on "Big Data" can be optimized by statistical and machine learning methods. The quality of the simulation can be evaluated by training the model on a piece of data. For example, by training a predictive model of evolution on time series until 2017, you can get the system forecasts for 2018, 2019, and subsequent years, and compare the forecast provided by the system with the real territorial development of the city in these years. A computing system based on such a model can be used to analyze and refine the city's development plans by comparing the development plan of an already developed city with the forecast of city development created based on previous development and the geographical characteristics of the earth's surface. A comparative analysis of these two spatiotemporal series of maps – "plans" and "forecasts" – can indicate possible planning shortcomings and suggest ways to eliminate them. The information system for forecasting the territorial development of cities, on which the provisions of this work will be illustrated, uses a computational model of the spatiotemporal evolution of cities, developed by the authors. Machine learning is very demanding on the quality of data, so in the course of the research, the authors paid great attention to data preprocessing (for methods of processing satellite data, see [1]).

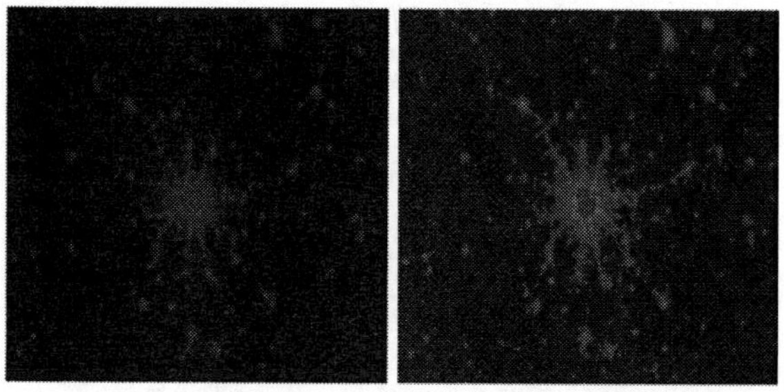

Figure 1: On the left – stable night-time lights of Moscow region in 2008. On the right – an urbanization map that was created based on these night-time lights.

Based on remote sensing data of the earth's night surface, the light footprints of cities are calculated. Night-time remote sensing data, in turn, allow calculating the so-called urbanization maps showing several levels of urbanization for a given city - the city center, nearby neighborhoods, and so on, a total of five levels. From these maps over several years, a time series of urbanization maps for a certain period is compiled.

Figure 1 features the stage of defining the boundaries of the compact residence of the population at a certain point in time. The time series of such maps allow for studying the territorial evolution of the city.

To model the dynamics of changes in this series, it is necessary to use physical characteristics of the earth's surface that hinder or contribute to the development in this area. These characteristics are extracted from the daytime multispectral satellite images. Machine learning can be useful at different stages of the system. For example, machine learning can be used to process space images to detect and classify the characteristics of the earth's surface and objects located on it (see, for example, [2]). In this work, the authors focus on the role of machine learning in optimizing model parameters and evaluating the quality of prediction results.

Figure 2 features an example of how the model calculating a forecast works. The top row shows urbanization maps for

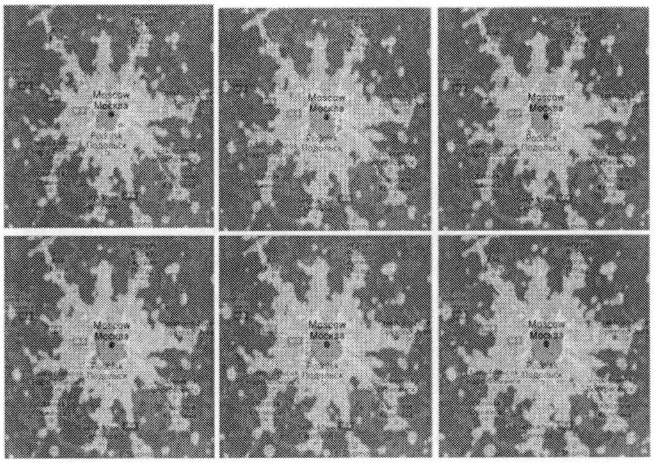

Figure 2: An example of calculating a forecast using semi-supervised learning based on data for Moscow.

2004, 2005, and 2006 (from left to right). The bottom row shows a forecast for 2007, 2008, and 2009 (from left to right). Such a forecast can be compared to real urban development to assess the quality of the forecast and adjust model parameters.

The urban growth model is an important tool for predicting and managing the expansion of cities. This paper discusses urban growth prediction using historical satellite data from the Defense Meteorological Satellite Program (DMSP) / Operational Linescan System (OLS) and Visible Infrared Imaging Radiometer Suite (VIIRS) / Day-Night Band (DNB). Nighttime DMSP and VIIRS data provide high-quality satellite images that capture the urbanization process over time. A machine learning optimization problem for the urban growth model based on the Probabilistic Cellular Automata (PCA) using historical satellite VIIRS data is also presented. The PCA is a popular method for modeling urban growth.

In particular, the well-known SLEUTH (slope, land-use, exclusion, urban extent, transportation, and hill shade) approach is also based on PCA (see [3]). The model was trained and its parameters were optimized with the help of historical VIIRS data. Different approaches to the solution of the optimization problem are also discussed in this paper.

The paper is organized as follows. Section II presents a short review of the urban growth predictive models based on machine learning. The authors' approach to the application of machine learning methods to urban growth is described in Section III. Section IV features the comparison of two predictive systems: the one developed by the authors and SLEUTH. Section V describes the advantages of the authors' system. Finally, Section VI concludes the paper.

II. Urban growth prediction and machine learning: outline

Urban growth models can be defined as spatiotemporal models, which can be generally grouped into three categories: (1) Cellular Automata (CA), (2) Agent-Based Models (ABM), and (3) Machine Learning models. Different machine learning algorithms have been used in the context of urban growth, including Logistic Regression (LR), Artificial Neural Networks (ANN), Linear Regression (LN), Decision Trees (DT), Random Forests (RFs), and so on.

In a systematic review of urban growth models in [10], their evolution, common frameworks, and applications were discussed. In particular, the review considered Cellular Automata models, Agent-based models, and Machine Learning models. In another review [7], it was demonstrated that RFs, Convolutional Neural Networks (CNN), and Support Vector Machines (SVM) are among the best algorithms for the classification and analysis of patterns in data obtained from earth observation as well as in urban growth problems. It was also emphasized that hybrid approaches combining machine learning and cellular automata have the potential for better performance in terms of accuracy, efficiency, and computational cost.

Machine learning techniques have been applied to different aspects of urban growth models, including calibration, sensitivity analysis, and validation. In [11], SVMs were applied to identify the most influential factors affecting urban growth in the federal state of North Rhine-Westphalia. The study found that land use change, population density, and road density were among the most important factors. In [12], an artificial neural network was used to develop an urban growth model for the five largest cities in Greece. The model incorporated various impact factors, such as social, economic, biophysical, neighboring-related, and political driving forces.

In [8], a novel technique combining supervised classification, prediction of urban growth, and machine learning was developed to predict urban growth boundaries and evaluate urban expansion. The technique showed that the expansion of Nasiriyah City was haphazard and unplanned, resulting in disastrous effects on urban and natural systems. In [9], Artificial Neural Network-Cellular Automata (ANN-CA) and Random Forest machine learning algorithms were used for urban growth modeling (2021–2041) in Islamabad, Pakistan. The study found that the city's urbanization has been unplanned and erratic, leading to dire consequences for the environment and urban systems.

Overall, machine learning techniques have shown promising results in improving the accuracy and efficiency of the SLEUTH model for urban growth prediction. However, more research is needed to further explore the potential of machine learning in this field.

III. Our application of machine learning methods to urban growth

The problem considered here is the prediction of the future growth of cities using PCA and historical satellite VIIRS data. Specifically, it is necessary to find the parameters of the PCA model that minimize the loss function, which measures the difference between the predicted urban growth and actual urban growth.

The optimization problem can be formulated as follows:

$$\underset{\theta \in \Theta}{\text{argmin}} \ \mathcal{L}(\theta), \tag{1}$$

where θ represents the model parameters, Θ is the parameter space, and $\mathcal{L}(\theta)$ is the loss function that measures the discrepancy between the predicted urban growth and the actual urban growth observed in the VIIRS data.

The loss function $\mathcal{L}(\theta)$ can be defined as the sum of two terms: a reconstruction loss $\mathcal{L}_{rec}$ and a regularization loss $\mathcal{L}_{reg}$. The structure of the reconstraction loss function in the area $\mathcal{A}$ is based on the mean squared error (MSE) between the predicted urban growth and the actual urban growth at each time step t :

$$\mathcal{L}_{rec}(\theta) = \frac{1}{nT} \sum_{x \in \mathcal{A}} w_i(t) \sum_{t=1}^{T} (y_{x,t} - \hat{y}(i_{x,t}; \theta))^2 \tag{2}$$

where n is the number of cells in the study area $\mathcal{A}$, T is the number of time steps, $w_x(t)$ is the weight assigned to cell x at time t, $y_{x,t}$ is the observed urban growth level at cell x and time t, $d_{x,t}$ is the input data at cell x and time t, and $\hat{y}(d_{x,t}; \theta)$ is the predicted urban growth level at cell x and time t based on the model with parameters θ.

The regularization loss $\mathcal{L}_{reg}$ penalizes the complexity of the model, and generally helps prevent overfitting. A common choice for $\mathcal{L}_{reg}$ is the L_2 norm of the parameters:

$$\mathcal{L}_{reg} = \lambda \cdot ||\theta||_2^2. \tag{3}$$

The motivation behind such a formulation of the problem is to develop a model that can accurately predict urban growth and be quite stable and robust. Urbanization is a complex process that involves various factors such as population growth, economic development, and land use change. Accurately predicting urban growth can help urban planners and policymakers make informed decisions regarding infrastructure development and resource allocation. Satellite VIIRS data is a rich source of information about night-time lights that provide unique information about population density. By leveraging this data, machine learning models can learn to identify patterns and predict urban growth with high accuracy.

To solve the optimization problem (1) efficiently, it is possible to use the stochastic gradient descent method (SGD) or one of its variants to update the parameters iteratively based on a minibatch of data. In particular, the optimization problem can be solved using gradient descent, which iteratively updates the parameters θ in the direction of the negative gradient of the loss function:

$$\theta_{t+1} = \theta_t - \alpha \nabla_\theta \mathcal{L}(\theta), \tag{4}$$

where α is the learning rate and $\nabla_\theta \mathcal{L}(\theta)$ is the gradient of the loss function with respect to the parameters θ.

The gradient of the loss function with respect to the parameters can be computed using backpropagation through the neural network. It is also possible to use such techniques as early stopping and learning rate scheduling to improve the performance of the model.

IV. Comparison of two predictive systems – ours and SLEUTH

The model developed by the authors of this paper uses a computational framework of probabilistic cellular automata: the earth's surface is divided into cells, the interactions of which are described by some rules. The evolution of cell states over time is modeled by discrete iterations of interactions according to these rules. The same scheme is used in the well-known SLEUTH model [3] [4].

SLEUTH is the most popular urban expansion model to date. The SLEUTH model reflects the patterns of urban expansion based on several input variables and is therefore relatively easy to understand. The interaction of different parameters of this model, as in any other cellular automaton, is based on explicitly described rules. It is important to note the already known shortcomings of SLEUTH (see [5]): adding new variables to the model and assessing their impact (e.g., beautification, land values, socio-economic distribution, access to utilities, etc.) are complex and time-consuming; the model considers only the fixed spatial neighborhoods of variables, although their spatial influence is not always the same; poor performance.

The authors expect that the use of their model will help to overcome the shortcomings of SLEUTH and will allow moving from "manual selection" of model parameters to their automated assessment, applying statistical and machine learning methods.

The SLEUTH system was developed and implemented in C programming language in the late 1990s. It is designed to model the spatial structure of land use changes. Since then, the system has practically not changed, having undergone only minor changes after 2001 (the last change was in 2017). It runs on a dedicated server and does not use parallelization technologies. The system is based on the use of cellular automata, which play a key role in it. The SLEUTH system uses cellular automata to model the spatial structure of land-use changes.

In general, working with the SLEUTH system is not an easy task, including compiling its source codes, configuring, preparing data, running diagnostics, analyzing calculation results, etc. Adding new modules to the SLEUTH system is also difficult, due to its monolithic architecture and underdeveloped diagnostics and I/O functions.

V. Advantages of our system

The prototype of the prediction module developed by the authors of this paper has been tested and has shown encouraging quality results.

The proposed system has demonstrated very good performance, thanks to the extensive use of parallelization of computing and cloud technology. Due to the use of modern architecture, this system is also easier to maintain and develop.

The performance of the system is very important, since the high speed of operation allows for conducting a large number of experiments with different data and various model parameters, and potentially opens up the possibility of using machine learning, which will improve the quality of predictions.

Our approach has significant advantages over the SLEUTH approach in terms of architecture, data used, model parameter settings, and the implementation of the model itself. Using the unique features of satellite data and cloud technologies, our model can provide faster and potentially more accurate forecasts of future territorial development.

At the architecture level, our system works in the cloud and uses all its advantages, such as high scalability, parallelization, the convenience of data storage, etc. The SLEUTH system, in turn, runs on a single dedicated server with a limited set of service functions and does not support parallelization. Thus, to increase the performance of SLEUTH, you need to upgrade the server at the physical level.

The authors use satellite data over different years, including "night lights" (DMSP, VIIRS), which provides several additional opportunities for forecasting territorial development. In particular, "night lights" help to reliably determine the boundaries of the compact residence of the population, as well as to estimate the population density. In contrast, SLEUTH relies on land-use maps and urbanization data, which may be outdated and incomplete.

Historical data also provides a unique opportunity to assess the quality of the predictive model and adjust additional global parameters of the model. The use of more extensive and diverse data sets allows for capturing changes over time better and providing more accurate forecasts of future development.

The model parameter settings in the approach developed by the authors differ from those used in SLEUTH. In the authors' implementation of integer automata, the history of changes in local data on the satellite data set used is taken into account. By evaluating the parameters based on this story, including the relationship between neighboring cells, the proposed model can better account for the complex and dynamic nature of urban development.

Effective application of machine learning and statistical methods is possible only if there is a large amount of data. The results of the work of "prediction" algorithms should be easily interpreted and credible. One can recall the statement of the economist J. M. Keynes where he claimed that the theory of probability for many "has a taste of astrology or alchemy" [6] (p. 8)). The same could be probably applicable to the results of machine learning. Therefore, in the developed information system, the initial focus is aimed at assessing the accuracy of projected urban sprawl maps using validation methods as well as visualizing the results at various stages of work.

The input data has spatial dimensions (latitude and longitude) and a temporal component (time or time interval). Localization by space allows considering the local characteristics of specific areas of interest and automatically adjusting the local parameters of the algorithms using machine learning. The presence of a time component in the data, in turn, allows making additional adjustments to the parameters based on historical data to improve the quality of the forecast and, where it is possible, to compare the forecast and the real development.

In the proposed system (see Figure 2), the main manipulated object is a time series of maps, where each pixel of data (correspondent to some area of the surface) is classified, for example, as "urban" or "non-urban". The classification is not binary but has several values corresponding to different ranges of population density in the corresponding area.

The Map Web application allows simultaneously visualizing different data layers and modeling results. Visualization, in turn, provides an opportunity to obtain, study, understand, and transfer to others difficult-to-formalize knowledge about the process of urbanization.

The software created by the authors allows:

- Creating and processing time series of two-dimensional data;
- Calculating the likely continuation for a given time series of data;
- Making joint calculations of several time series (in particular, calculating a binary measure of the similarity of two series of data cards.

As applied to the problem of spatiotemporal modeling of cities, the functions mentioned above allow:

- Preparing data;
- Training and calculating the forecast;
- Visually comparing the forecast obtained after training on historical data with the real development by calculation;
- Calculating a measure of the quality of the forecast, which provides an opportunity to directly improve the parameters of the forecast calculation algorithm;
- Conducting a comparative analysis of "plans" made by policymakers and "forecasts" computed by the proposed system.

The authors believe that a new round of progress in the field of predictive computing systems for the territorial development of cities will occur primarily due to the improvement of nonfunctional characteristics, such as the simplicity of data preparation, system performance, visualization efficiency, and the ease of results interpretation at various stages of work. Assessing the quality of modeling by training a model on a piece of data at an early stage of system development helps to improve the model and quantify the usefulness of certain data. The use of the new model allows shifting from the manual selection of model parameters to the selection of real data on the territorial development of cities. The growing flow of new instrumental data and data from techno-social systems, such as social networks, will soon provide a substantial improvement in the quality of forecasting with the help of statistics and machine learning.

VI. Conclusion and Future Work

This paper is aimed at considering the issues related to the application of machine learning in designing and creating predictive models for the territorial development of cities. The use of satellite data in developing machine learning predictive models is also discussed. The role and importance of remote sensing data, particularly night lights VIIRS/DNB satellite data, in the development of these models, is highlighted. Additionally, the authors share their experience in developing an information system for forecasting the territorial development of cities based on remote sensing satellite data.

Furthermore, a novel approach to developing a mathematical model for urban growth prediction is presented. This approach is based on machine learning using VIIRS/DNB satellite data. The corresponding optimization problem for finding optimal parameters of the urban growth predictive model is also raised and discussed.

In the future, the authors plan to carry out practical experiments involving urban growth predictive models in real-world urban planning scenarios. To evaluate the performance of the urban growth predictive model, quantitative metrics will be employed to compare the predicted values with the actual observed values using historical satellite data. These metrics will provide a clear indication of how well the model aligns with the observed urban growth in diverse real-world scenarios. In particular, the Root Mean Square Error (RMSE) metric will be used. By analyzing and comparing the RMSE values across different regions and time periods, a comprehensive assessment of the model's accuracy can be made, allowing for the identification of potential variations in its performance. Furthermore, the authors intend to employ validation techniques, such as cross-validation, to thoroughly assess the robustness and generalizability of the model.

REFERENCES

[1] M. Zhihin and A. Troussov, "Applied tasks of remote sensing of the Earth's night surface," Publishing House 'Delo', 2021, 159 pages., ISBN: 978-5-85006-311-5. (In Russian).

[2] A. Troussov, D. Botvich, and S. Vinogradov, "Detection of Gas Flares Using Satellite Imagery," PATTERNS 2021, The Thirteenth International Conference on Pervasive Patterns and Applications (Porto, Portugal, April 18-22, 2021), 2021, pp. 45-49.

[3] K. C. Clarke, S. Hoppen, and L. Gaydos, "A self-modifying cellular automaton model of historical urbanization in the San Francisco Bay area," Environ. Plan. B Plan. Des., 24, 1997, pp.247–261.

[4] K. C. Clarke and L. J. Gaydos, "Loose-coupling a cellular automaton model and GIS: Long-term urban growth prediction for San Francisco and Washington/Baltimore," Int. J. Geogr. Inform. Sci. 1998, 12, 1998, pp. 699–714.

[5] J. A. Gomez, J. E. Patino, J. C. Duque, and S. Passos, "Spatiotemporal Modeling of Urban Growth Using Machine Learning," Remote Sensing, vol. 12, no. 1, 2020, pp. 109-119.

[6] H. Cramer, "Special invited paper. Half a century with probability theory: some personal recollections," The Annals of Probability, Vol. 4, No. 4, 1976, pp.509–546.

[7] V. Chaturvedi and W. T. de Vries , "Machine Learning Algorithms for Urban Land Use Planning: A Review," Urban Science, vol. 5, no. 3, article no. 68, 2021.

[8] S. K. Hanoon, A. F. Abdullah, H. Z. M. Shafri, and A. Wayayok, "Urban Growth Forecast Using Machine Learning Algorithms and GIS- Based Novel Techniques: A Case Study Focusing on Nasiriyah City, Southern Iraq," ISPRS International Journal of Geo-Information, 12(2), 76, 2023.

[9] A. Khan and M. Sudheer, "Machine learning-based monitoring and modeling for spatio-temporal urban growth of Islamabad," The Egyptian Journal of Remote Sensing and Space Science, vol. 25, no. 2, 2022, pp. 541-550.

[10] X. Li, Y. Chen, X. Chen, and Y. Wang, "Urban growth models: progress and perspective," Science Bulletin, vol. 61, no. 21, 2016, pp. 1637-1650.

[11] A. Rienow and R. Goetzke, "Supporting SLEUTH – Enhancing a cellular automaton with support vector machines for urban growth modeling," in Computers, Environment and Urban Systems, vol. 49, 2015, pp. 66-81.

[12] P. Tsagkis, E. Bakogiannis, and A. Nikitas, "Analysing urban growth using machine learning and open data: An artificial neural network modelled case study of five Greek cities," Sustainable Cities and Society, vol. 89, 2023, p. 104337.

Best Practices (and Stumbling Blocks) for Diversity-Sensitive Behavior Change in Persuasive Application Design

Alexander G. Mirnig
AIT Austrian Institute of Technology
Center for Technology Experience
Vienna, Austria
alexander.mirnig@ait.ac.at

Stefan Eibl
University of Applied Sciences Wiener Neustadt
Campus Wieselburg
Wieselburg, Austria
stefan.eibl@fhwn.ac.at

Thomas Poscher
University of Applied Sciences Wiener Neustadt
Campus Wieselburg
Wieselburg, Austria
thomas.poscher@fhwn.ac.at

Lisa Diamond
AIT Austrian Institute of Technology
Center for Technology Experience
Vienna, Austria
lisa.diamond@ait.ac.at

***Abstract*—Design for Behavior Change can be used to enact changes on an individual basis or beyond to gradually modify users' behaviors and constituting attitudes towards achieving a desired goal. Today, achieving more sustainable behaviors is a frequent goal of behavior change apps found on the market. In order to be effective across a wide and diverse spectrum of users and simultaneously avoid stigmatization or marginalization, the design of such applications should be done in a diversity-aware manner, which is often still lacking. In this paper, we present a best practice analysis of existing applications in the domains of food consumption, mobility, and energy consumption that are available on the market in Austria, Europe. We present the findings as a collection of three design patterns and discuss their status as patterns versus anti-patterns in terms of how well diversity factors are implemented in existing practice and where improvements are necessary.**

***Index Terms*—behavior change, sustainability, diversity, design patterns.**

I. Introduction

Behavior change support systems can be employed to modify users' attitudes and behaviors in consideration of individual motives, living contexts, and other individual or user-specific factors. Today, such support systems are mainly available in the form of apps that can be deployed across devices (typically with smartphones and tablets the primaries, web and desktop secondaries) to enable access to and continuous use of the system.

The climate crisis constitutes one of the most relevant target domains for behavior change [1]. A limiting factor of behavior change effectiveness in this domain is an often insufficient regard for gender and diversity aspects [2] in behavior change support systems, which can cause disengagement from using such systems and exclude groups of individuals from using them [3].

In order to close this gap, the project *biscuit4all* [4] investigates gender- and diversity appropriate design for behavior change support systems in the climate-relevant application domains mobility, nutrition, and energy consumption. In this paper, we present the results from a best practice analysis of behavior change in the Austrian (EU) market (Section III) condensed into brief design patterns (Section IV) that show best practices as well as areas for improvement (Section V) to achieve better behavior change successes.

II. Related Work

Theories of behavior change typically focus on behavioral intention accompanied by other core variables concerning conditions, habits, beliefs, responsibility perceptions and other components. Commonly applied theories and models include Triandis' theory of interpersonal behavior [5] with attitude, social factors, affect and frequency of past behavior impacting intention and habits. Ajzen's theory of planned behavior [6] considers attitudes, norms and perceived behavioural control as core components. Stern et. al's value-belief-norm theory [7] builds on values (biospheric, altruistic and egoistic), beliefs and personal norms. Challenging factors that can pose issues in the context of behavior change towards sustainability are cognitive limitations, insufficiently perceived personal relevance and missing tangibility, distrust and reactance [8].

Persuasive approaches such as the persuasive strategies discussed by Oinas-Kukkonen and Harjumaa [9] and Fogg [10] offer the possibility to directly address important factors of behaviour change and overcome some of these barriers. Common approaches include providing information that underlines the responsibility and agency of the individual, accurate feedback and social feedback to increase literacy and correct self-serving and in-group biases, by offering timely and location-specific prompts to battle bad habits and help with limited cognitive resources.

Gender and other diversity dimensions including age and class impact a number of factors important for sustainable behaviour changes, such as attitudes and intentions or habits in connection with societal roles. Women typically show, for example, more positive attitudes towards sustainable behaviour [11], different types of sustainable behaviour [12], [13], which are also shaped through gender roles and access to free time and resources that come with them [14], [15], and more sustainable behaviour overall [16], [17]. We can also see gender differences with regards to the type of values that motivate behaviour [18].

Higher Income households typically have higher carbon footprints [19], [20] but also more resources for high impact changes. Both income and age-related differences can also be seen in attitudes with younger people indicating to care more about climate change [21] and being more likely to cycle [22], and older people being more inclined to purchase food locally [23]. The middle class is more likely to show sustainable behaviour than the upper or lower class [24] but class associations with particular activities, such as cycling, also impact willingness to adopt behaviours [25]. These observed differences change the persuasive effect of different approaches to engagement strategy design and highlight the importance of gender and diversity-sensitive design of behaviour change support apps.

In their review paper from 2016, Thomson, Nash, and Maeder [26] identified and collected a number of issues in implementations of behaviour change techniques and persuasive design principles in physical activity smartphone applications. A lack of support for the diversity of user needs and preferences was highlighted as one of the main issues identified, alongside information flow and presentation, user engagement and retention, and a generally fragmented use of persuasive principles.

Design Patterns were originally conceived by Christopher Alexander [27], [28] for capturing solutions in Architecture and were later introduced for use in Software Engineering by Gamma et al. [29]. Distinguishing features of patterns are capturing of contextual information, problem focus, and the potential to capture implicit knowledge [30], [31], [32]. They are also used in Human-Computer Interaction to capture and communicating working solutions [33] and constitute an effective way to capture a design state-of-the art in a way that enables immediate reproduction to the pattern reader. To address issues outlined by Thomson, Nash and Maeder, the patterns presented in this paper draw from best practices in diversity-sensitive design [2] for personalisation, feedback design, and user engagement.

III. Best Practice Analysis

The screening process and best practice analysis of behavior change support apps followed procedures outlined in previous content analyses of mobile apps [34], [35]. In January 2023, the iOS App Store and the Android Play Store were screened for relevant apps using smartphone devices. Only apps that were free of cost were included in the analysis, as previous studies suggest that users are reluctant to pay for apps and prefer apps that are free of cost. We focused on analyzing apps from three specific categories related to behavior change support that are relevant for climate change: food consumption, energy, and mobility.

To identify best practice examples in our study, we employed a two-step screening process. First, we searched for apps that had been mentioned in reputable journal and magazine rankings, indicating their recognition within the field. Second, the thusly selected apps underwent a meta-analysis that took factors such as the number of downloads, ratings, and the level of star ratings into account. The operationalization of the best practice analysis was conducted using a deductive categorization approach based on content analysis. Predefined categories and characteristics of best practices were established. Based on these criteria, the identified apps were systematically analyzed and evaluated. The deductive approach allowed for a structured and targeted analysis of the apps to identify potential best practices. Apps lacking these functionalities were automatically excluded from our analysis.

The screening process began by defining keywords relevant to the selection of journals and magazines. Since the research focused on German speaking locations, we conducted the screening process on the basis of German keywords. For the "food consumption" category, we utilized keywords such as "Besser Essen Apps" (Better Eating Apps), "Lebensmittel retten" (Food Rescue), "Ernährung" (food consumption / nutrition), and "Ernährung verändern" (Changing food consumption). For "energy," we used keywords such as "Energie Apps" (Energy Apps), "Energiesparen Apps" (Energy Saving Apps), "Stromsparen Apps" (Electricity Saving Apps), "Energieeffizienz" (Energy Efficiency), "Gas sparen Apps" (Gas Saving Apps), and "Heizkosten sparen" (Save Heating Costs). For "food consumption" we utilized keywords such as "Besser Essen Apps" (Better Eating Apps), "Lebensmittel retten" (Food Rescue), "Ernährung" (food consumption / nutrition), and "Ernährung verändern" (Changing food consumption). Through this initial search, we identified 105 food consumption apps, 119 mobility apps, and 54 energy apps. Via an inclusion criterion of needing to be mentioned in reputable journals or magazines at least 7 times, we narrowed down the selection to 8, 15, and 8 apps, respectively. Subsequently, we applied exclusion criteria that filtered out apps available only in the paid version, with less than 1000 ratings, and with less than 4-star ratings in the respective app store. We also employed forward and backward snowballing techniques based on in-app-store recommendations to potentially identify additional relevant apps. The screening process led to the identification of a total of 6 food consumption, 7 mobility, and 7 energy apps for further analysis.

The content analysis of the identified apps was conducted to gain insights into their features and functionalities. For the systematic analysis, we derived the categories to be examined from the work of Oinas-Kukkonen & Harjuuma

[9]. For each app, we extracted information on the each of the following categories: reduction, tunneling, tailoring, personalization, self-monitoring, simulation, rehearsal, praise, rewards, reminders, suggestion, similarity, liking, social role, trustworthiness, expertise, surface credibility, real-world feel, authority, third-party endorsers, verifiability, social learning, social comparison, normative influence, social facilitation, cooperation, competition, recognition, gender&diversity.

IV. PATTERNS

The results from the best practice analysis served as the basis for the design patterns, which were generated using the general structure outlined by Mirnig et al. [36]. An additional mining step was performed to consolidate the identified practices per each of the categories by Oinas-Kukkonen & Harjuuma [9], and then formulate an application domain independent description that summarizes the underlying solutions. The categories represented in the patterns were chosen based on the common issues of behavior change systems outlined by Thomson, Nash, and Maeder [26], which also served as the primary inspiration for the problem statements. This matching eventually resulted in three patterns for personalization techniques, feedback tangibility, and effective tunneling. We should note at this point that diversity-sensitive design was usually a by-product and rarely the focus in the identified practices. As a result, the mining focused on directly diversity-sensitive or diversity supporting design. In the following, we present the initial version of all three patterns using the reduced structure by Mirnig et al. [37] in order to suit the publication format.

A. Pattern 1: Personalization Techniques for Diversity Integration

This pattern describes solutions to enable users to fit the app output and or general UI to their personal needs under specific consideration of gender- and diversity-related factors. This cannot only improve the interaction quality but also make app interaction and output more appropriate and better usable within a user's individual situation.

1) Problem: If a user's needs, preferences and abilities are not adequately considered when designing a behaviour change app, then successful usage of the app and adherence to interventions on the user side will be limited [26].

Generalized (i.e., non-personalized) cues, reminders, or entire routines are unlikely to fit every user's context. As a result, system output might mismatch in terms of the user's goals or be inappropriate regarding the user's living situation. Furthermore, either through use of the app or a change in circumstances unrelated to the app, the user can be expected to change and modify their goals, needs, and preferences accordingly. This, in turn, will result in previously effective techniques to no longer be (as) effective and/or established routines or programs to no longer be appropriate.

2) Solution: In order to appropriately reflect and support within a user's individual situational context, behaviour change success can be enabled via:

1) custom goal setting,
2) diversity-sensitive personalization,
3) personalization effects.

Custom goal setting allows the user to define their goals on two levels:

- qualitative, and
- quantitative.

The *qualitative* level specifies the general target that is to be achieved. Sustainability-related and other typical targets are "eat less meat", "reduce food waste", and "lose weight" in food consumption, "fastest connection", "cheapest connection", or "lowest carbon emission connection" in mobility, and "reduce consumption" or "achieve target consumption" in energy. Additional targets depend on app purpose and intended user group. For food consumption, targets to include or exclude based on dietary requirements or preferences (e.g., celiac, vegetarian, vegan – ideally with a default preset and additional customization to specify included and excluded food categories) are recommended. Mobility can similarly allow to set a preference for (or exclude) certain types of mobility means or routes to accommodate motion sickness or sustainability concerns. In Energy, personalization can be tied to actions and events tied to the overall energy consumption. Example factors here are number of laundries done within a period, laundry temperature, or number of hot beverages consumed within a certain period.

The *quantitative* level allows the user to define a specific quantitative target on the previously defined qualitative level. Suitable units for quantities depend on the use case but "cost in [currency]" is commonly sensible across all three target domains. The carbon footprint is commonly used in Energy and Mobility but can serve in food consumption as well when a user wants to additionally tailor their consumption with sustainability in mind. The quantitative level should be addressed with both predefined goals or suggestions as well as customizability of quantities. It is important that a user can customize on both levels and in the order of quality $\rightarrow$ quantity. Presets that stop at the qualitative level or that do not allow full quantitative customization run the risk of not addressing user contexts appropriately.

Diversity-sensitive personalization allows a user to personalize the app and its output in accordance with their individual situation. This is commonly achieved via tying personalization-specific settings to a user profile, so that this step does not need to be repeated unless necessary (i.e., when circumstances change and the user wishes to change their settings). Best practices in diversity-sensitive personalization are still limited, though common settings include age, language, and gender.

Diversity is not limited to the common factors listed above. Financial situation is an important diversity factor and must be addressed in order to avoid exclusionary design. While this factor is partially addressed via goal setting, further integration is important to avoid unintended side effects. E.g., if an app categorizes consumption or prices into cheap/medium/expensive, then these categories need to reflect the general economic situation within the user's economic environment as well as what constitutes cheap vs. expensive within the user's individual situation. Financial situation can be made an explicit value (e.g., enter monthly income and expenses), though care should be taken to not make users uncomfortable or stigmatize if social comparison techniques are also employed. If possible, financial situation should be implemented as a derived value and compare goal settings to local averages; explicit definition should be optional.

The personalization can only be effective if it is tied to actual **personalization effects**. Diversity-sensitive personalization effects should go beyond cosmetics and either impact the successful interaction with the app itself or the generated app output. For the former, font size and colour contrasts need to be customizable to accommodate preferences and disabilities. If and wherever possible, cues, notifications, and general output should be customizable regarding modes (visual, auditory, haptic; inclusion of 'silent' modes) in order to accommodate different daily situations and disabilities.

Customization choice can be reflected visually to communicate to the user that certain settings are currently active. Nonfunctional and overbearing visuals should be avoided. E.g., a user enters 'woman' as a gender in the profile and is then presented with a bright pink theme serves no functional purpose while potentially stigmatizing and repelling the user from further interacting with the app. In addition, defaults should be chosen carefully, e.g., when languages are tied to location settings. In places with several active and/or official languages, it is recommended to let the user immediately specify their primary language after setting the location instead of assuming the standard language and making the user change it post-hoc via the settings page.

Personalization effects must be communicated to the user. This can be done via tooltips when editing the profile, or as part of other information messages during loading or idle periods. Wizards, if employed, should lead the user through the settings and explain the effect of each setting on the respective page. It is important that the explanations are not limited to the wizard alone and can still be accessed when a user decides to update their settings afterwards outside the wizard.

3) Examples: The apps *YAZIO* [38] and *MyFitnessPal* allow personalization regarding age, language, and sex (see Figures 1 and 2). Tooltips explain the effects of each setting. In *YAZIO*, sex choice is reflected via different (gender-switched) images throughout the rest of the interaction process to increase relatability. This example limits the gender choice to only two, which should be avoided in order to not exclude users beyond the binary spectrum.

MyFitnessPal [39] uses a wizard to collect user preferences in terms of their perceived level of activity to match and customize recommended activities and levels of intensity (see Figure 3.

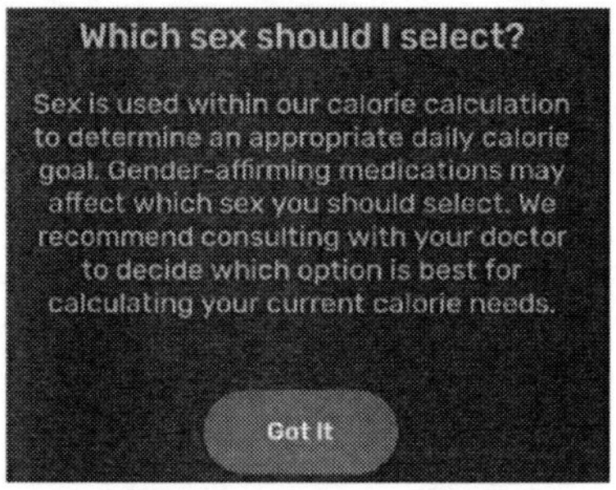

Fig. 1. Example for sex choice explanation from *YAZIO*.

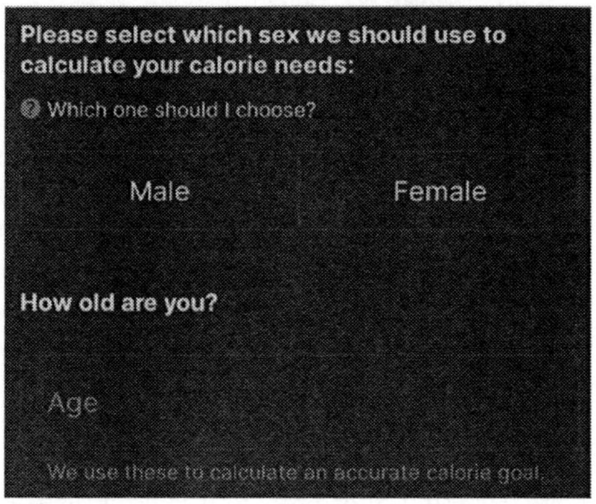

Fig. 2. Example for sex choice, age setting, and explanation of their effects from *MyFitnessPal*.

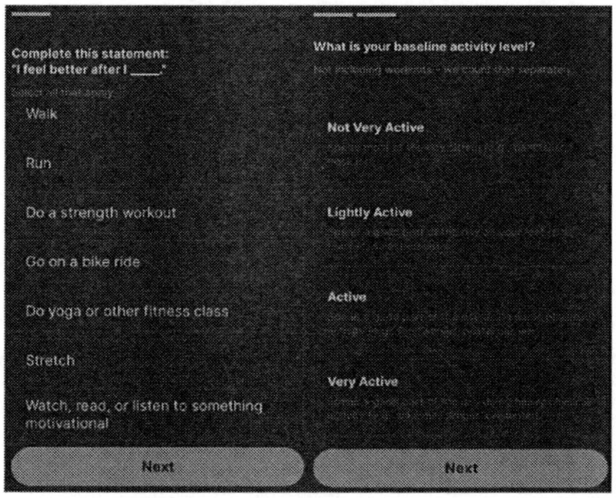

Fig. 3. *MyFitnessPal* asks for user's estimated level of activity after the user specified their desired activity type.

B. Pattern 2: Tangible Feedback Design

This pattern describes solutions to frame the app output in a user intelligible manner. This ensures that the previously diversity-tailored persuasive content is appropriately received and fully processed by the user, increasing its effectiveness.

1) Problem: Presentation and flow of the information the user receives should be intelligible and simple to comprehend [26]. If the presented information does not fit into the user's current frame of reference, then additional translational steps are required in order to accurately process the information presented. If this is not provided via the app or cognitively done by the user, the app and its employed strategies can be expected to be less effective. If the additional translation for comprehension needs to be done by the user, then using the app becomes more cumbersome, reducing usability and likelihood of user retention over time.

2) Solution: The feedback by the system must be such so that it is **tangible** to the user. 'Tangible' in this context is to be understood that the user can associate an immediate meaning to a given piece of information and situate it within their frame of reference.

In order for a value to be tangible, unit and magnitude need to be understood by and, if necessary, explained to the user. E.g., an isolated carbon footprint value can be difficult to comprehend without any additional information. Bringing it into context with items the user is familiar with enables framing and referencing. In the concrete example, a user could be presented with the carbon footprint of brewing a cup of coffee as an isolated value. The daily/weekly/etc. average carbon footprint per person/household/etc. within the user's country or region can be used to serve as global reference for the provided value. In addition, the footprint of, e.g., driving their car for 100kms / their daily commute / etc. can further contextualize the action in relation to their other known activities, thus rendering it intuitively graspable and easy to comprehend.

Tangibility is also achieved by allowing a user to monitor and compare current values or behaviours to past as well as future (projected) instances. Thus, *longitudinal information output*, e.g., in form of a histogram or similar visualizations, adds tangibility in terms being able to relate current data points to previous ones and easily see increases, decreases, deviations, and the like. Lastly, additional tangibility can be achieved by enabling intuitive qualitative goals, as described in Pattern 1. If users can tailor their goals not just towards units that they can intuitively comprehend but further into units that they interact with in everyday life (e.g., glasses of water consumed, nr. of gas tank refills, etc.), tangibility of information presentation is increased, leading to more direct engagement with the app.

3) Examples: The food app *Lifesum* [40] enables goals to not only be set towards calories but additionally tracks carbohydrates, proteins, and fats separately. Further tangibility is added by tracking hydration goals (overall indication in litres) via glasses of water consumed (see Figure 4). Additional tangibility is achieved via statistical overview of past food consumption behaviour, a so-called "LifeScore", which provides a single-number approximation regarding how healthy/unhealthy the current eating habits are, and tracking of streaks. Streaks (i.e., periods of uninterrupted goal achievement) provide an easy way to track own achievements in a simple number format and allow historical contrasting via comparison of current to recorded highest streak.

Histograms and similar overviews are commonly used particularly in Energy apps and provide reference to contrast daily with periodic consumption and plan actions to achieve goals accordingly. The *AVA-App* [41] can not only show data on past consumption but also has indicators to denote the price range within that period. The app differentiates on three levels between expensive, medium priced, and low priced, which further aid the user to assess their consumption in relation to costs and can be used for more informed forecasting as well. It has to be noted, though, that while the assessment of whether a price is expensive or not can be done in relation to market highs, lows, and averages, what a user considers expensive will ultimately depend on their disposable income. Thus, such margins are ideally customizable to fit the user's individual situation.

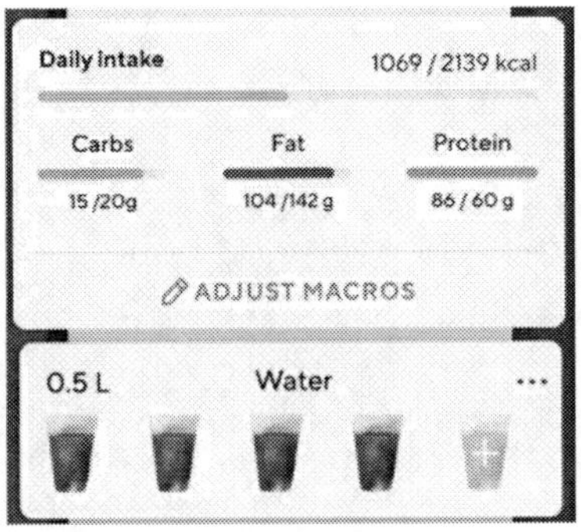

Fig. 4. Separation of intake into carbohydrates, proteins, fats (and respective maximum values) and water tracker from *Lifesum*.

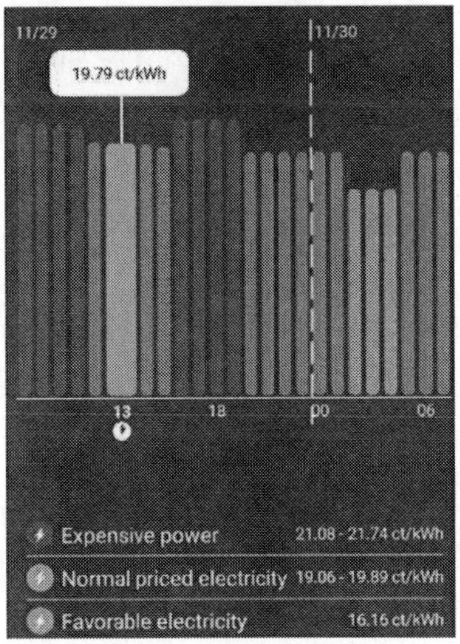

Fig. 5. The *AVA App* labels values in its consumption histogram in relation to how (in)expensive the price per kWh can be considered to be.

C. Pattern 3: Maintaining User Engagement via Effective Tunneling

This pattern describes solutions to increase user engagement and retention via tunneling strategies.

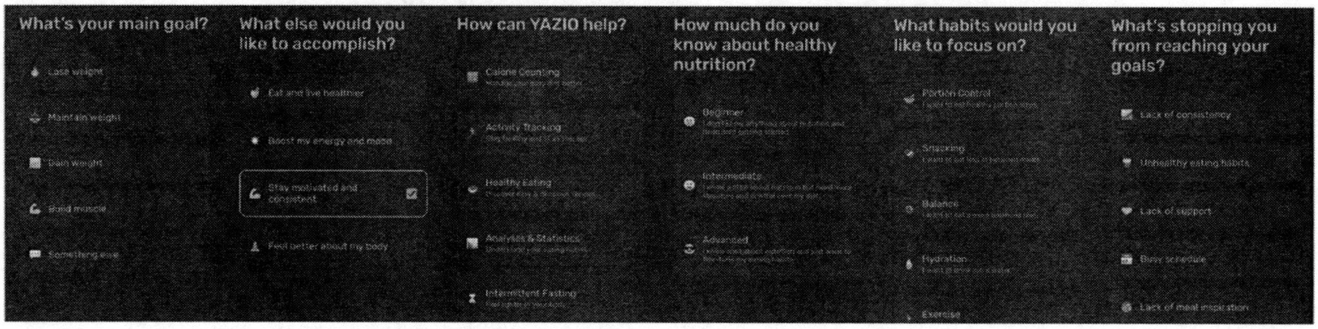

Fig. 6. The Wizard of the app *YAZIO* tunnels effectively by asking the user's goals in steps and additionally captures their nutritional knowledge and impeding factors.

1) Problem: Behaviour change is a continuous process. As a consequence, in order for behaviour change apps to be effective, users need to stay engaged in using the app for an extended amount of time so that a lasting impact on their behaviour can actually manifest. If there is insufficient motivation for a user to keep returning to the app beyond initial use, then the likelihood of impactful app use is low. Even more critical are cases where apps repel users from repeated use due to cumbersome navigation, convoluted interfaces, or lengthy input sequences before each use. Such obstacles need to be minimized in order to retain user engagement and ensure user retention.

2) Solution: Tunneling is a strategy that can be employed to lower the input barrier of complex or multi-step processes, thus making them easier to handle and reducing the workload on the user. Tunneling refers to guiding the user through predetermined sequences of actions instead of giving them free reign over all functionalities from the get-go. This means that users need to give up a certain extent of freedom of interaction and engage with parts of the system or engage in tasks they might not otherwise have engaged in.

This has two important benefits: Since the tasks as well as the ranges of possible tasks per step are pre-defined, the complexity can be controlled and the interaction designed so as to not overwhelm the user at any given point. Any complex or lengthy process can be segmented into individually manageable sequences via tunneling. The second benefit is that users are more likely to commit to completing a sequence to completion once they have begun engaging in it. Thus, tunneling can be used to both lower the initial entry barrier and keep the user engaged throughout the app use.

Effective tunneling means knowing when to employ tunneling, since the user will not always be willing to have their freedom of choice reduced. Two fitting spots for tunneling are: At the *first* start of using an app and at the start of a new activity (task or info query). The former is usually handled via Wizards, which help users set up the necessary profile data in order to effectively start using the app.

When designing a startup-Wizard, it is important to delineate the strictly necessary from the optional information. During interaction with the Wizard, the user should always be informed, what the information provided or setting chosen will impact and whether a step can be skipped. The initial tunneling should be kept flexible, so that the user can either skip parts of the initial sequence or cancel it altogether and still engage with the app on some level. They should also have the opportunity to re-start the Wizard at any point in order to complete their setup (or review information they require a refresher on).

Pre-activity tunneling means that whenever a user decides to begin a new activity, they are presented with a number of predefined options and are then efficiently guided via a sequence consisting of several choices. A well-established solution is to follow a question-based approach. The first question should ask the user what they want to achieve on a general level (e.g., save money, maintain weight, reduce gas consumption, eat more sustainably, etc.). The subsequent questions should then allow them to specify how they want to achieve their goal (by indicating tasks/activities they want to do *or* by having them explicitly exclude activities they do not want to perform or know to not work for them from past experiences). The final step should then allow them to set their goals and should always be in the form of modifiable suggestions, so that the user can tailor if and when desired.

In the context of competency building as important component of sustainable behaviour support, tunneling can be employed to provide pre-selected choices for areas of behavioural adjustment or accordingly tailored actionable advice.

3) Examples: The food consumption app *YAZIO* tunnels the user effectively upon initial use by using a Wizard and following the goal-based question approach (see Figure 6). The app tunnels effectively by asking primary and secondary goals and then presents the app functionalities and brief explanations on how each one can assist to achieve the user's goals. The query on healthy food consumption knowledge is well-positioned and is not something a user easily or immediately divulges on first use but can be used by the app to calibrate the amount of info output in the following steps. Focus on habits and explication of impeding factors help to further tailor the suggested tasks. This allows the generation of a very detailed and customized task profile with an interaction flow that never exceeds a complexity of a six choice maximum presented to the user.

V. Discussion

In the following, we discuss the identified solutions, existing best practices, and areas for improvement for each pattern.

A. Personalization

With regards to qualitative personalization, it is important to design options under consideration of diversity-specific needs. For food consumption these include in example elements such as limited budget in the context of income, and/or time for food purchase e.g., in relation to living phase and family situation and preparation. In the context of mobility, traveling with little children and with safety concerns which more often affects women, status-related motivations which we see more often with men, and with limited mobility as can be relevant for the elderly and disabled but also people with care responsibilities are some of the aspects to consider. Regarding energy consumption relevant limitations to consider are e.g., availability for load shifting in relation to employment status, life phase and gender as women often bear the main share of housework and are also more often at home with young children, as well as limited resources and possibilities in relation to income, class and geographical location which are also associated with household equipment, dwelling type and ownership.

Of further importance on the quantitative level is sufficient granularity for captured characteristics that e.g., avoids capturing gender only as binary variable and takes the age of children in the household into consideration. This is specifically important in the context of ensuring the inclusion of marginalized groups such as non-binary users. Options for quantitative consumption should be designed with comprehensibility and personal relevance for different user groups in mind. Even seemingly very generalized translations, such as energy as travel distance by car or hours watched on a TV, could be less accessible for people who do not own cars or TVs.

B. Tangibility of Feedback

Presentation and flow (as well as quantitative goalsetting from pattern 1) should not be in isolation and always stay tied to user-specific motivations. Regarding timing, whether a prompt is considered "timely" will differ between different user groups, e.g., with regards to how much need to plan ahead is needed and how "immediate" their possibility to interact with the app is when a notification has been sent.

Suggestions for actions need to be strongly tied to possibilities and there need to be ways to specify that specific types of actions are not possible such as cycling due to a disability, buying bulk due to food-related intolerances that do not allow for contamination or using the tumble dryer less often if there is insufficient space available to air-dry all laundry.

With any sort of visualization to provide feedback comprehensibility for different user groups also needs to be taken into consideration and different forms should be provided if needed. These forms, as other personalization options should be developed under involvement of a diverse user group to avoid the designer's specific understanding and context to shape the app to a degree that excludes potential user groups.

C. Tunneling

With tunneling it is particularly important to ask the right questions that allow an understanding of given motivations, abilities, and limitations with a diversity-sensitive approach so that it can be employed in an effective manner but without removing choices needed to indicate diversity-related conditions. Similar considerations apply to tunneling of action-related choices and and information that aim at building literacy and competency. Particular care should therefore be applied in the implementation.

More emphasis is needed on what the right time for which type of assessment is. If users are confronted with one question after another that they do not see relevant at that time, there is a real risk of repelling them. If, however, the question is woven into a task-specific interaction tunnel, then answering a diversity-relevant question will be a logical and intuitively graspable part of the interaction flow. A similar approach has been suggested for communicating privacy-relevant information [42]. Some practices exist on when to ask for sex, gender, age, economic status but a more structured understanding when and where to place which diversity-factor assessment is required to better support tunneling within and across the application domains.

VI. Conclusion and Future Work

In this paper, we presented three design patterns for diversity-sensitive design of behaviour change systems. These patterns are based on results from a best practice analysis of existing applications in the domains of nutrition, mobility, and energy consumption on the Austrian market. The best practices condensed into pattern solutions were chosen such so that they match stated issues that inhibit the success of behavior change support systems. The identified best practices can not yet be considered comprehensive and often lack in explicitly targeting diversity and are rather general design practices that can also be used to support diversity-aware design. When diversity is directly addressed, only a rather narrow range of relevant-factors is currently considered. Including a wider range is necessary to render in- as well as output naturally tied to diversity factors instead of having them "tacked on". We were able to identify a number of concrete areas for advancement for all three patterns and will further pursue refinement of the pattern solutions in order to arrive at comprehensive and actionable guidance for diversity-sensitive behavior change system design.

Acknowledgment

The financial support by the Austrian Federal Ministry for Climate Action, Environment, Energy, Mobility, Innovation and Technology through the Austrian Research Promotion Agency (FFG) under grant number FO999892826 (Project: biscuit4all) within the program "FEMtech" is gratefully acknowledged.

References

[1] R. Pachauri and L. Meyer, "Climate change 2014: Synthesis report. contribution of working groups i, ii and iii to the fifth assessment report of the intergovernmental panel on climate change," Online, 2014, IPCC, Geneva, Switzerland. [Online]. Available: https://www.ipcc.ch/report/ar5/syr/

[2] J. Himmelsbach, S. Schwarz, C. Gerdenitsch, B. Wais-Zechmann, J. Bobeth, and M. Tscheligi, "Do we care about diversity in human computer interaction: A comprehensive content analysis on diversity dimensions in research," in *Proceedings of the 2019 CHI Conference on Human Factors in Computing Systems*, ser. CHI '19. New York, NY, USA: Association for Computing Machinery, 2019, p. 1–16. [Online]. Available: https://doi.org/10.1145/3290605.3300720

[3] E. Dowler, S. Turner, B. Dobson, and C. P. A. G. G. Britain), *Poverty Bites: Food, Health and Poor Families*, ser. Poverty publication. Child Poverty Action Group, 2001. [Online]. Available: https://books.google.at/books?id=fE-FAAAAIAAJ

[4] "biscuit4all," 2023, Project Website, URL: https://biscuit4all.info/ [accessed: 15-05-2023].

[5] H. Triandis, *Interpersonal Behavior*. Brooks/Cole Publishing Company, 1977. [Online]. Available: https://books.google.at/books?id=Sz63AAAAIAAJ

[6] I. Ajzen, *From Intentions to Actions: A Theory of Planned Behavior*. Berlin, Heidelberg: Springer Berlin Heidelberg, 1985, pp. 11–39. [Online]. Available: https://doi.org/10.1007/978-3-642-69746-3_2

[7] P. C. Stern, T. Dietz, T. Abel, G. A. Guagnano, and L. Kalof, "A value-belief-norm theory of support for social movements: The case of environmentalism," *Human ecology review*, pp. 81–97.

[8] K. S. Wolske and P. C. Stern, "Contributions of psychology to limiting climate change: Opportunities through consumer behavior," in *Psychology and climate change*. Elsevier, pp. 127–160.

[9] H. Oinas-Kukkonen and M. Harjumaa, "A systematic framework for designing and evaluating persuasive systems," in *Persuasive Technology*, ser. Lecture Notes in Computer Science, H. Oinas-Kukkonen, P. Hasle, M. Harjumaa, K. Segerståhl, and P. Øhrstrøm, Eds. Springer Berlin Heidelberg, no. 5033, pp. 164–176. [Online]. Available: http://link.springer.com/chapter/10.1007/978-3-540-68504-3_15

[10] B. J. Fogg, *Persuasive Technology: Using Computers to Change What We Think and Do*. Morgan Kaufmann, google-Books-ID: r9JIkNjjTfEC.

[11] D. Costa Pinto, M. M. Herter, P. Rossi, and A. Borges, "Going green for self or for others? gender and identity salience effects on sustainable consumption," *International Journal of Consumer Studies*, vol. 38, no. 5, pp. 540–549.

[12] B. Bloodhart and J. K. Swim, "Sustainability and consumption: What's gender got to do with it," *Journal of Social Issues*, vol. 76, no. 1, pp. 101–113.

[13] L. M. Hunter, A. Hatch, and A. Johnson, "Cross-national gender variation in environmental behaviors," *Social science quarterly*, vol. 85, no. 3, pp. 677–694.

[14] R. Räty and A. Carlsson-Kanyama, "Energy consumption by gender in some european countries," *Energy Policy*, vol. 38, no. 1, pp. 646–649.

[15] J. Fathallah and P. Pyakurel, "Addressing gender in energy studies," *Energy Research & Social Science*, vol. 65, p. 101461.

[16] Z. A. Bulut, F. Kökalan Çımrin, and O. Doğan, "Gender, generation and sustainable consumption: Exploring the behaviour of consumers from Izmir, Turkey," *International Journal of Consumer Studies*, vol. 41, no. 6, pp. 597–604.

[17] L. C. Zelezny, P.-P. Chua, and C. Aldrich, "Elaborating on gender differences in environmentalism," *Journal of Social issues*, vol. 56, no. 3, pp. 443–458.

[18] S. H. Schwartz and T. Rubel, "Sex differences in value priorities: cross-cultural and multimethod studies." *Journal of personality and social psychology*, vol. 89, no. 6, p. 1010.

[19] J. Wilson, P. Tyedmers, and J. E. Spinney, "An exploration of the relationship between socioeconomic and well-being variables and household greenhouse gas emissions," *Journal of Industrial Ecology*, vol. 17, no. 6, pp. 880–891.

[20] M. Sommer and K. Kratena, "The carbon footprint of european households and income distribution," *Ecological Economics*, vol. 136, pp. 62–72.

[21] T. L. Milfont, E. Zubielevitch, P. Milojev, and C. G. Sibley, "Ten-year panel data confirm generation gap but climate beliefs increase at similar rates across ages," *Nature Communications*, vol. 12, no. 1, p. 4038. [Online]. Available: https://www.nature.com/articles/s41467-021-24245-y

[22] S. Kaplan, D. K. Wrzesinska, and C. G. Prato, "The role of human needs in the intention to use conventional and electric bicycle sharing in a driving-oriented country," *Transport policy*, vol. 71, pp. 138–146.

[23] F. Bimbo, C. Russo, A. Di Fonzo, and G. Nardone, "Consumers' environmental responsibility and their purchase of local food: evidence from a large-scale survey," *British Food Journal*, vol. 123, no. 5, pp. 1853–1874.

[24] L. Yan, H. T. Keh, and J. Chen, "Assimilating and differentiating: The curvilinear effect of social class on green consumption," *Journal of Consumer Research*, vol. 47, no. 6, pp. 914–936. [Online]. Available: https://doi.org/10.1093/jcr/ucaa041

[25] M. Anantharaman, "Elite and ethical: The defensive distinctions of middle-class bicycling in Bangalore, India," *Journal of Consumer Culture*, vol. 17, no. 3, pp. 864–886.

[26] C. Thomson, J. Nash, and A. Maeder, "Persuasive design for behaviour change apps: Issues for designers," in *Proceedings of the Annual Conference of the South African Institute of Computer Scientists and Information Technologists*, ser. SAICSIT '16. New York, NY, USA: Association for Computing Machinery, 2016. [Online]. Available: https://doi.org/10.1145/2987491.2987535

[27] C. Alexander, *The Timeless Way of Building*. New York, USA: Oxford University Press, 1979.

[28] C. Alexander, S. Ishikawa, and M. Silverstein, *A Pattern Language: Towns, Buildings, Construction*. New York, USA: Oxford University Press, 1997.

[29] E. Gamma, R. Helm, R. Johnson, and J. Vlissides, *Design Patterns: Elements of Reusable Object-Oriented Software*. Pearson Education, 1994.

[30] G. Meszaros and J. Doble, "Pattern languages of program design 3," R. C. Martin, D. Riehle, and F. Buschmann, Eds. Boston, MA, USA: Addison-Wesley Longman Publishing Co., Inc., 1997, ch. A Pattern Language for Pattern Writing, pp. 529–574.

[31] J. Vlissides, *Pattern Hatching: Design Patterns Applied*. Addison-Wesley, 1998.

[32] M. V. Welie and G. C. V. D. Veer, "Pattern languages in interaction design: Structure and organization," in *Proc. Interact '03, M. Rauterberg, Wesson, Ed(s). IOS*. IOS Press, 2003, pp. 527–534.

[33] J. O. Borchers, "A pattern approach to interaction design," *AI & SOCIETY*, vol. 15, no. 4, pp. 359–376, 2001.

[34] K. Kalke, T. Ginossar, J. M. Bentley, H. Carver, S. F. A. Shah, and A. Y. Kinney, "Use of evidence-based best practices and behavior change techniques in breast cancer apps: Systematic analysis," *JMIR Mhealth Uhealth*, vol. 8, no. 1, p. e14082, Jan 2020. [Online]. Available: https://mhealth.jmir.org/2020/1/e14082

[35] T. Ginossar, S. F. A. Shah, A. J. West, J. M. Bentley, C. A. Caburnay, M. W. Kreuter, and A. Y. Kinney, "Content, usability, and utilization of plain language in breast cancer mobile phone apps: A systematic analysis," *JMIR Mhealth Uhealth*, vol. 5, no. 3, p. e20, Mar 2017. [Online]. Available: http://mhealth.jmir.org/2017/3/e20/

[36] A. G. Mirnig et al., "User experience patterns from scientific and industry knowledge: An inclusive pattern approach," *International Journal On Advances in Life Sciences*, vol. 7, no. 3 and 4, pp. 200–215, 2015. [Online]. Available: https://www.thinkmind.org

[37] A. G. Mirnig, P. Fröhlich, J. Schrammel, D. Falcioni, M. Gafert, and M. Tscheligi, "Pattern languages in interaction design: Structure and organization," in *Proceedings of The Twelfth International Conference on Pervasive Patterns and Applications (PATTERNS 2020)*. IARIA, 2020, pp. 63–69.

[38] "YAZIO," 2023, YAZIO Gmbh, URL: https://www.yazio.com/ [accessed: 15-05-2023].

[39] "MyFitnessPal," 2023, MyFitnessPal, Inc., URL: https://www.myfitnesspal.com/ [accessed: 15-05-2023].

[40] "Lifesum," 2023, Lifesum AB, URL: https://lifesum.com/ [accessed: 15-05-2023].

[41] "AVA App," 2023, Salzburg AG, URL: https://www.ava-assist.me/ [offline as of 30-05-2023], Apple Store: https://apps.apple.com/at/app/ava-energy-assistant/id1545318042, Play Store: https://play.google.com/store/apps/details/AVA_Energy_Assistant?id=com.salzburgag.digitallab.stromzeiten&gl=US&pli=1 [accessed: 15-05-2023].

[42] L. Diamond and P. Fröhlich, "Communicating privacy: User priorities for privacy requirements in home energy applications," in *Human-Computer*

Interaction – INTERACT 2021, C. Ardito, R. Lanzilotti, A. Malizia, H. Petrie, A. Piccinno, G. Desolda, and K. Inkpen, Eds. Cham: Springer International Publishing, 2021, pp. 665–675.